# Scot and Irish Ancestors
## of
## Kenneth McAffee
## Ralston

Harold A Ralston

# Scot and Irish Ancestors
# of
# Kenneth McAffee Ralston

**And**
**His Forebears-**
**Ralston, McAffee, Cross, Brown, Greenlee,**
**McCarty, & Benedict**

**With Pictures, Charts, and Maps**

©Harold A Ralston
Mt Pleasant, WI
March 2020

ISBN 978-1-67815-195-9
Lulu Publishing
lulu.com

# Pedigree Chart

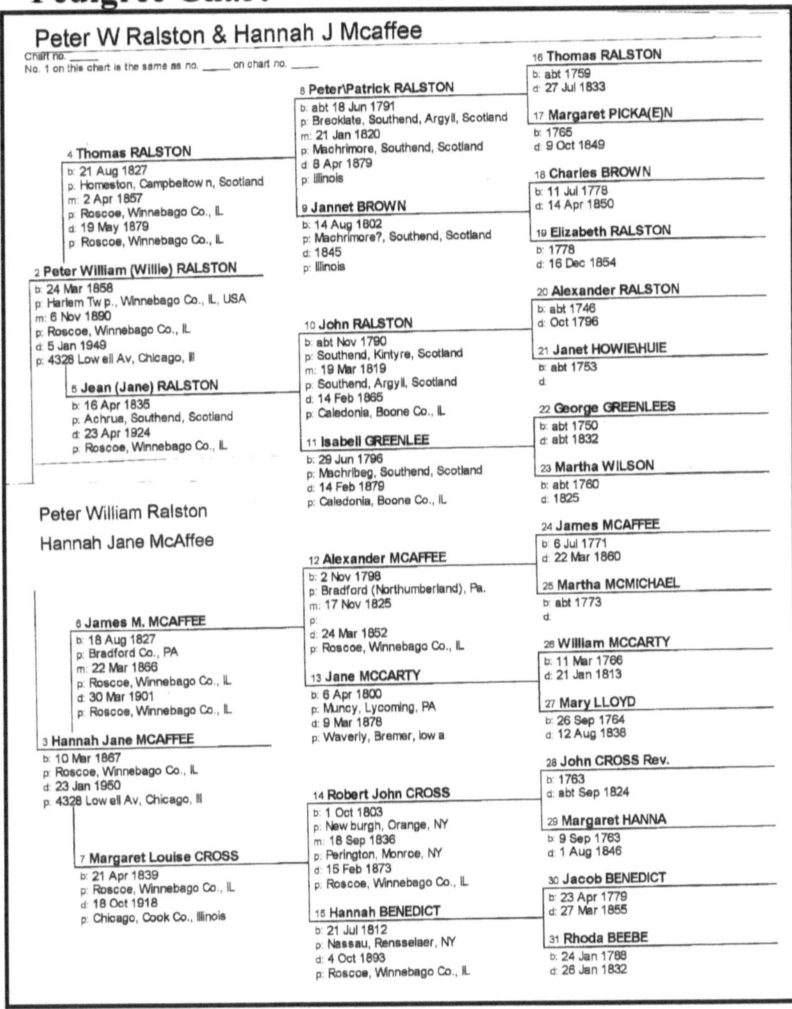

## Peter W Ralston & Hannah J Mcaffee

Chart no. _____
No. 1 on this chart is the same as no. _____ on chart no. _____

**2 Peter William (Willie) RALSTON**
b: 24 Mar 1858
p: Harlem Twp., Winnebago Co., IL, USA
m: 6 Nov 1890
p: Roscoe, Winnebago Co., IL
d: 5 Jan 1949
p: 4328 Lowell Av, Chicago, Ill

Peter William Ralston

Hannah Jane McAffee

**3 Hannah Jane MCAFFEE**
b: 10 Mar 1867
p: Roscoe, Winnebago Co., IL
d: 23 Jan 1950
p: 4328 Lowell Av, Chicago, Ill

**4 Thomas RALSTON**
b: 21 Aug 1827
p: Homeston, Campbeltown, Scotland
m: 2 Apr 1857
p: Roscoe, Winnebago Co., IL
d: 19 May 1879
p: Roscoe, Winnebago Co., IL

**5 Jean (Jane) RALSTON**
b: 16 Apr 1835
p: Achrua, Southend, Scotland
d: 23 Apr 1924
p: Roscoe, Winnebago Co., IL

**6 James M. MCAFFEE**
b: 18 Aug 1827
p: Bradford Co., PA
m: 22 Mar 1866
p: Roscoe, Winnebago Co., IL
d: 30 Mar 1901
p: Roscoe, Winnebago Co., IL

**7 Margaret Louise CROSS**
b: 21 Apr 1839
p: Roscoe, Winnebago Co., IL
d: 18 Oct 1918
p: Chicago, Cook Co., Illinois

**8 Peter\Patrick RALSTON**
b: abt 18 Jun 1791
p: Brecklate, Southend, Argyll, Scotland
m: 21 Jan 1820
p: Machrimore, Southend, Scotland
d: 8 Apr 1879
p: Illinois

**9 Jannet BROWN**
b: 14 Aug 1802
p: Machrimore?, Southend, Scotland
d: 1845
p: Illinois

**10 John RALSTON**
b: abt Nov 1790
p: Southend, Kintyre, Scotland
m: 19 Mar 1819
p: Southend, Argyll, Scotland
d: 14 Feb 1865
p: Caledonia, Boone Co., IL

**11 Isabell GREENLEE**
b: 29 Jun 1796
p: Machribeg, Southend, Scotland
d: 14 Feb 1879
p: Caledonia, Boone Co., IL

**12 Alexander MCAFFEE**
b: 2 Nov 1798
p: Bradford (Northumberland), Pa.
m: 17 Nov 1825
p:
d: 24 Mar 1852
p: Roscoe, Winnebago Co., IL

**13 Jane MCCARTY**
b: 6 Apr 1800
p: Muncy, Lycoming, PA
d: 9 Mar 1878
p: Waverly, Bremer, Iowa

**14 Robert John CROSS**
b: 1 Oct 1803
p: Newburgh, Orange, NY
m: 18 Sep 1836
p: Perington, Monroe, NY
d: 15 Feb 1873
p: Roscoe, Winnebago Co., IL

**15 Hannah BENEDICT**
b: 21 Jul 1812
p: Nassau, Rensselaer, NY
d: 4 Oct 1893
p: Roscoe, Winnebago Co., IL

**16 Thomas RALSTON**
b: abt 1759
d: 27 Jul 1833

**17 Margaret PICKA(E)N**
b: 1765
d: 9 Oct 1849

**18 Charles BROWN**
b: 11 Jul 1778
d: 14 Apr 1850

**19 Elizabeth RALSTON**
b: 1778
d: 16 Dec 1854

**20 Alexander RALSTON**
b: abt 1746
d: Oct 1796

**21 Janet HOWIE\HUIE**
b: abt 1753
d:

**22 George GREENLEES**
b: abt 1750
d: abt 1832

**23 Martha WILSON**
b: abt 1760
d: 1825

**24 James MCAFFEE**
b: 6 Jul 1771
d: 22 Mar 1860

**25 Martha MCMICHAEL**
b: abt 1773
d:

**26 William MCCARTY**
b: 11 Mar 1766
d: 21 Jan 1813

**27 Mary LLOYD**
b: 26 Sep 1764
d: 12 Aug 1838

**28 John CROSS Rev.**
b: 1763
d: abt Sep 1824

**29 Margaret HANNA**
b: 9 Sep 1763
d: 1 Aug 1846

**30 Jacob BENEDICT**
b: 23 Apr 1779
d: 27 Mar 1855

**31 Rhoda BEEBE**
b: 24 Jan 1788
d: 26 Jan 1832

# Contents-


Pedigree Chart ........................................................ 1

Contents- ............................................................... 3

Introduction- .......................................................... 5

A Question ............................................................. 7

Kenneth McAffee Ralston and Evelyn Belden ............... 9

Thomas Ralston and Jane (Jean) Ralston- ................... 21

Peter Ralston and Jannet/Janet Brown ....................... 25

John Ralston and Isabell Greenlee/s ........................... 27

James McAffee and Margaret Cross- ........................... 29

Alexander McAffee and Jane McCarty ......................... 35

Robert Cross and Hannah Benedict ............................ 39

Kenneth Ralston and Evelyn Belden- Cousins ............. 45

Pictures- ................................................................ 47

Kenneth McAffee Ralston sketches- about 1914 ........ 97

Farm Scenes- .......................................................... 99

Documents- ............................................................ 110

Artifacts- ............................................................... 130

Maps- .................................................................... 136

Robert J Cross Park and Home ................................. 149

My other books ....................................................... 153

# Introduction-

This second edition replaces the first one that was printed in June 2014. Family history information has been expanded and Cross Park in Roscoe and a Kintyre Old Parish Record copy are added. Thanks to cousin Connie for the pictures from the family album in her possession.

It was originally published to provide a record, and identification when possible, of the collection of Ralston family pictures and studio portraits. In order to help with the identification, I included some of the family history and genealogy.

**This history starts with Kenneth McAffee Ralston's parents**.

Kenneth's parents, Peter William Ralston and Hannah Jane McAffee were born Winnebago County, Illinois. He in Harlem Township and she in Roscoe Township, about two miles apart.

P. Wm.'s parents came to Illinois from Scotland.

- His father, Thomas Ralston with parents and family, came to Illinois in 1843. Thomas was age 15. They left Kintyre Scotland on the British Barque "*Tay*" in 1840 and spent time in Ohio on the way.
- His mother Jane Ralston and family came to Illinois from Scotland in 1850. Jane was age 16. Her parents with family traveled from Scotland on the ship "*Charlotte Harrison*".

⚹

Hannah's ancestors were from Ireland and England and had been in New York, Pennsylvania and Michigan prior to coming to Illinois.

- Her father, James M McAffee, came with his parents and family to Illinois in 1839 from Pennsylvania.

- Her mother Margaret Louise Cross was born in Roscoe, Illinois in 1839.
- Her Grandfather Alexander McAffee was born in Towanda, Pennsylvania in 1798 and came to Roscoe, Illinois in 1839.
- Her Grandmother Jane McCarty McAffee was born in Muncy, PA and came to Roscoe with Alexander in 1839.
- Her Grandfather Robert J Cross came to Roscoe in 1835 from Michigan. Robert was born in Newburgh, NY.
- Her Grandmother Hannah Benedict Cross was born in Nassau, NY in 1812 and came to Roscoe in 1836 following marriage to Robert J Cross.
- Her Great Grandfather James McAffee was born in 1771 and died in 1860 in PA.
- Her Great Grandmother Martha McMichael McAffee was born about 1773 in Pennsylvania.
- Her Great Grandfather William McCarty was born in Bucks Co., PA in 1766 and died in Muncy, PA in 1813.
- Her Great Grandmother Mary Lloyd McMichael was born In Bucks, PA in 1764 and died in Muncy, PA in 1838.
- Her Great Grandfather John Cross was born in Northern Ireland in 1760 and came to NY with parents about 1798.
- Her Great Grandparents Rev. John Cross and Margaret Hanna lived in Northern Ireland before leaving for Orange Co., NY about 1798.
- Her Great Grandfather Jacob Benedict was born in Nassau, NY in 1779 and died in Perinton, NY in 1855,.
- Her 7th great grandfather Thomas Benedict came from England to NY about 1648.
- Her Great Grandmother Rhoda Beebe Benedict was born in 1788 in Manchester, VT and died January 26, 1832, burial in Fairport, NY near the Erie Canal..

# A Question

## I wonder how Grandma Hannah McAffee Ralston's grandparents first met.

Both, Robert J Cross and Hannah Benedict, were born in NY State.

It seems that she was born in 1812 at Nassau, Rensselaer Co. He was born in 1803 at Newburgh, Orange Co. About 80 miles along the east bank of the Hudson River.

The Benedict family came from England about 1638. John Benedict was on Long Island, NY when he married in 1670. Benedict ancestors were living in Connecticut for a time before Hannah Benedict's father Jacob was born in Nassau, New York. Jacob was probably living in Perinton, Monroe Co., NY when he died in 1855. He is buried in Greenvale Rural Cemetery there near the Erie Canal by Rochester, NY.

The Cross family came from Ulster (Northern Ireland) Ireland to NY City about 1798 and after a short stay moved to Newburgh where Robert was born. His brother, William was born in Bethel, Sullivan Co. where they were living at that time. They were living in Bloomfield, Ontario Co., when their father John Cross died in 1824. In 1825, Robert and William claimed land in Tecumseh, Lenawee Co., MI and the two of them moved there in 1826.

In 1836 Robert traveled to Wisconsin and Illinois where he obtained land along the Rock River in Rock Co., WI and Winnebago Co., IL. He settled in Roscoe along the Rock River and was living there when he went back East in September 1836 to marry Hannah Benedict at Perrington, Monroe Co., NY.

Based on this information, it does not seem likely that they had met in NY since there homes were not located close.

There are a few clues however.

Hannah Benedict's younger sister, Cornelia, was married to Isaac Coles of Rockton, IL in May of 1836, just four months before Hannah and Robert were married.

Hannah's younger brother, John, "left NY for Clinton Junction, WI where he built a log cabin." This would have been within ten miles of where Robert Cross lived.

James Benedict, another brother, was also near Clinton, where he was a charter member of the Clinton Junction Congregational Church. Thomas and Charles Tuttle were church founders there and Thomas donated land for a church building.

Rev. Albert Tuttle organized a Wesleyan Church in Roscoe where he was an early settler. The Methodist Church founders in Roscoe, IL included Albert and Amos Tuttle in 1837.

***Did Robert J Cross and Hannah/Susannah Benedict meet in NY or WI before they married, or did they become acquainted through correspondence?***

# Kenneth McAffee Ralston and Evelyn Belden

**Kenneth McAffee and Evelyn Emma Blanche Belden Ralston**

Kenneth McAffee Ralston, born 21 November 1895 in Chicago, Illinois, was the second son of Peter William and Hannah J. McAffee Ralston. He attended Chicago schools and at about age 19 went to work on his Grandmother's farm on McDonald Road near Roscoe. While in school he attended Schurz High School and the Chicago Art Institute. As a child he sold newspapers on street corners, probably on Montrose Avenue. It had street-car stops with people going to or returning from work. The family lived nearby at 4328 Lowell Avenue.

Although Kenneth had not completed high school, he was a very progressive farmer and a leader in community and church affairs. He constantly read of the latest agricultural practices in farm journals and put them into practice. He was among the first in the county to adopt the testing of butterfat content and weight of milk produced in order to determine which cows were the most productive. As soon as it was available, he adopted the use of artificial insemination as a method for improving the young stock added to the herd. He converted the horse stall area of the barn to provide for a total of about 30 milking cows. He made a practice of purchasing young beef cattle from Western cattle growers and fed them corn, hay and cottonseed cake protein supplement in order to fatten for market. Before livestock trucks became commonly available he herded the cattle to the railroad siding in Roscoe for shipment to the stockyards in Chicago. He accompanied them by riding in the caboose of the freight train for the overnight trip. The commission men working for the Chicago Livestock Producers Association would sell them, of which he became a Board Member in later years. He also purchased Western lambs for fattening and shipping to the Chicago stockyard. They were purchased in the fall and pastured on the fields where they could make use of grain that was missed in the harvesting operations. He raised hogs for market. They would be kept in the same feedlot as the cattle in order to make use of the grain that passed through without being fully digested. He vaccinated and castrated the young pigs with the help of a hired man and his sons. He had several hired men over the years prior to when the sons were able to provide substantial help. One of the last was his brother Bill. When Bill married and started farming on his own, one of his wedding gifts was a workhorse from Kenneth.

He was a stickler for keeping records and using figures. He kept very complete records of every expenditure whether for farm business or home. As an early participant in the Farm Bureau Farm Management service, he kept detailed farm business records for over 25 years. His wife, Evelyn, did the same for the home management. It was common for him to record in his little pocket diary the cost of meals at a restaurant, whether paid by him or others. He had a desire to have an accounting of every cent spent. This practice of recording economic data greatly assisted in his understanding of the profit and loss of the enterprise and the parts of the farm operation that were not profitable indicating the need for changes or modification.

He had a strong sense of punctuality. This meant preparing ahead of time to be ready so that last minute flurry of activities was unnecessary. For example shine shoes the night before so that they were all ready for Sunday school rather than waiting until the last minute. This sense of punctuality resulted in a need for schedules. A schedule was significant and in the later years became of greater importance so that he was prepared for an event since it took a little longer to get ready.

One of his great interests over the years was baseball, not just watching, but also playing. He was a lifelong fan of the Chicago White Sox baseball team, not withstanding their scandal in 1919. This is of interest since he was born and grew up on the near-north side of Chicago, not far from the Cubs Park. There were many years when an automobile trek from Roscoe was made to see one or more baseball games in Chicago. It would often be for a double header on Sunday. That way you got the most for your money. It was quite a sacrifice since it meant getting back late for evening chores and milking the cows. He played baseball for a local sandlot team as catcher for recreation, probably on weekends. He followed closely the athletic pursuits of all his children, and when possible, his grandchildren and great grandchildren. He participated with them and the nieces and nephews on the home front lawn on many a Sunday afternoon during family gatherings, right up until the last decade. He mostly pitched, encouraging the batters and chastising the fielders for poor plays. He played basketball as a school board member (1936-1943) during their challenge by the faculty as an opener to the high school season.

He was an active member in many organizations- the Winnebago County Farm Bureau (Charter Member and Director), Winnebago County Farm Service Company, Pecatonica-Durand Soil Conservation District (Director). He was among the first to adopt contour strip farming of crops and to build water control terraces on his farm in order to control soil erosion. He used soil-building practices such as spreading limestone to control acidity, spreading potash, phosphate, and ammonia nitrate to increase available plant food in the soil. He rotated his crops, planting oats, alfalfa, alfalfa, and corn in a four-year cycle to maintain humus and fertility levels. The Governor of Illinois appointed him to the State Soil Conservation Board. In 1949 he received a national soil conservation award in Des Moines, Iowa. He served the ASCS as County Committeeman, was a director of the Midwest Dairyman's Association, was active in Winnebago County Extension Service, served as elected member and President of the Harlem Consolidated School District board, a Trustee of the Harlem-Roscoe Fire Protection District, and Life Member of the Lovejoy School Parents Teachers Association.

He served as trustee of the Argyle Scottish Cemetery. He was a member of the Roscoe Grange and a member of the Harlem Historical Society. He was a member and Elder of the Willow Creek Presbyterian Church and active on many committee functions. He was a member of The Northwest Gun Club and a winner of the annual shoot more than once. In his retirement years, he was a member of the Roscoe Young at Heart Club.

Following his years of active farming, he was elected to the position of Township Assessor, Harlem Township and held it for fourteen years. He died 9 September 1991 after a short illness, at the Alpine Fireside Health Center, Rockford.

On 15 June 1922 Kenneth married Evelyn Emma Blanche Belden at the home of her parents on Elevator Road in Roscoe, Illinois. They lived their entire married life on the Ralston farm on McDonald Road near Roscoe. They had seven children: Elizabeth A, Russell B, Laurence E, Harold A, David C, Mary Jane and Duane K.

Evelyn Emma Blanche Belden was born 15 February 1902 at Honey Creek, Wisconsin.

*Honey Creek--A fine eight pound girl was born to Mr. and Mrs.* Louis Belden *on Saturday morning last. It is a beauty of a girl and may be in the baby show next fall.*

*Honey Creek Happenings-Born to Mr. and Mrs. Louis Belden, a daughter.*

*Honey Creek- Mrs. Ella Belden of Rochester spent Sunday with her son Louis and wife. She came to see the baby.*

*Honey Creek--Louis Belden has moved his wife, his baby and himself into the Dame house. Mr. B. will be employed with Mr. B. Rose the coming season.* (Plat map of B. Rose farm)

She moved with her parents to Rockford, Ill., and then, moved to Tom Miner's place, from there to farm of C. A. Glenny, in 1907, east of Roscoe, then to O. Manley Farm, in 1908, then to Andrew Roth farm, in 1910. The next move, in March, was to the McAffee house across from the Roscoe School. She went to school one year at Booth School. The rest of schooling was at Roscoe. She graduated from 2 year Roscoe High School in 1918. The graduating class consisted of two students.

According to her autobiography she worked some at Rockford Overall factory, staying at Grandma Goff's, then advanced to the Wholesale Grocery, collecting orders before shipping to stores. Evelyn took a course at Beloit Business College, and worked for her board caring for Bobby at R. L. Newfield home *(January 1920 Federal census shows her, age- 17, with LeRoy Newfield- 28, wife, Rose- 26, and son Robert-31/2 in Beloit, Rock Co., WI)* She had a short job at Chamber of Commerce. She then filled in at Iron Works a short time and, worked some time at Bicknell Supply & Co. on So. Broad Street.

Later she was placed at J. H. Patterson in Roscoe with R. H. Perkins, Mgr., and her father, working there. It was while employed here that her future husband first saw her when he came into the office on farm business. Asa Taylor later became Mgr. She quit working there a short time before marriage.

Evelyn was an active member of the Willow Creek Presbyterian Church, in Argyle, Winnebago County Homemakers, and Double Seven Sunday School Class. She was active in church Women's Circle and as Sunday School Teacher.

Evelyn lived her entire married life on the Ralston Farm southeast of Roscoe. She died at age 83, on the morning of 3 October 1985 at home. Pastor Steven Plank at Delahanty Funeral Home, Loves Park and at graveside, Scottish Cemetery, Argyle, conducted services.

Evelyn was married on 15 June 1922 to Kenneth McAffee Ralston at her home on Elevator Road in Roscoe. Pastor was Rev. Floyd A. Kufus, Bridesmaid was Alice A. Belden and Groomsman was Donald McColl. They traveled on a honeymoon to the Grand Hotel at Janesville and on to Wisconsin Dells at the Crandall Hotel. They took both the upper and lower Dells river trips and motored by taxi to Mirror Lake and Devil's Lake. They visited P. W. Ralston's in Chicago and took a Lake Michigan boat trip to St. Joseph, Mich. from Chicago.

Peter William Ralston and Hannah Jane McAffee -

Peter William Ralston.

**Hannah Jane McAffee**

Peter was the first child of Thomas Ralston and Jean Ralston, born 24 March 1858 on the family farm in Harlem Twp., Winnebago Co., Illinois.

He attended local schools, probably in Harlem. Had good attendance record and seldom missed a day at school. He was handy with carpenter tools and had a wooden pot that he used when going to Roscoe for sugar (Now in possession of Great Grandson; Robert W Ralston). Was allergic to horse hair but farmed until brother John was old enough to take over the farm. Joined Northwest Gun Club, Argyle, soon after it was formed in 1877.

On 17 June 1890, at age 32 he graduated from Beloit College Academy in the field of English. The graduation exercises included talks by eight class members, a debate by two others and music by a duet and the Class Banjo Club. An academy bulletin described the Business, or English course of study as "meets the wants of those not looking forward to a College course, but wishing those studies helpful to an entrance upon business life or teaching." According to the academy grade ledgers, he attended during; Winter, Spring and Fall terms of 1887, Winter and Spring terms of 1888, Fall term of 1889, and Winter and Spring terms of 1890. The ledger shows his grades in: Grammar, Arithmetic, Physiology, Business Arithmetic, Elementary Rhetoric, Botany, Algebra, Physical Geography, Zoology, Chemistry, German,

Biology, Roman History, English Classics, and Physics, etc., (some are too light to read), with Declamations, Essays and Bible Study throughout the courses. The complete curriculum was three years, Junior, Middle, and Senior. Expenses are listed as "Tuition, Fall Term, 15 weeks...$10.00, Winter and Spring Terms...$8.00. Rent of rooms (furnished with stoves) in College Buildings, is from $10 to $20 per year. Board and room in private families is from $3.75 to $5.00 per week."

He married Hannah J. McAffee, daughter of James McAffee and Margaret Cross, on 6 November 1890 in her parents Roscoe home, located on the farm originally settled by Robert J. Cross in 1835. The house is still standing on Hononegah Road.

They soon moved to Chicago where he was engaged in engineering work for various firms. One was the Chicago and Northwestern Railroad. His work was not steady and sometimes took him out of town. He helped layout several streets in the city and was working on a railroad project in Upper Michigan in late 1918. The railroad, from St. Ignace to Sault Ste. Marie however, was not built on that site. Chicago home was near Lincoln Park for a short time and then in Avondale but later had a house built in Irving Park by his brother-in-law Earnest Worcester (husband of Julia McAffee), about 1897-8. It was in a new area at 4328 Lowell Avenue. Earnest was paid $2 a day plus $1 a day for an assistant.

'Willie' had belonged to Willow Creek Presbyterian Church in Argyle. He later joined Irving Park Methodist church. Perhaps because there was no Presbyterian Church in the area. He was on the Church Board and active in the Men's Bible Class. He was a poll worker during election times. He enjoyed gardening, hoeing, weeding and raising vegetables.

In letters sent to Kenneth Ralston between June and October 1918, he describes some of the work he was doing for the railroad while based at Antigo, Wisconsin. On June 16, he was at Antigo staying at the Hoffman House Hotel and had been to Rhinelander and New London the previous week and was going to Oshkosh the following day. July 17 he was at Monico lining curves and would go 70 miles north the following day. On Aug. 20, he was 20 miles N. E. of Antigo. On September 25, he had been 28 mi. south of Antigo at Eldora doing a survey for logging purposes. On the way up from Chicago that week, there was a freight wreck north of Split Rock so the train backed up to Clintonville and then up another line to Shawano and up to Eland Jct. to return to the main line. While at Shawano he saw a large crowd listening to a speaker and nearby there was a train with 3 French 77's, a German trench mortar and a wrecked Fokker plane. He had gone to Wausau in the afternoon and would go to Appleton the next day to layout a new roundhouse. On October 9 he was near Marshfield and would go to New London the following day.

P. William Ralston died at his Chicago home 5 January 1949. "*Peter W. Ralston. Caledonia- Peter W. Ralston, 90, died yesterday afternoon at his home in Chicago. He had been in good health until shortly before he died. Peter Ralston was born in Harlem Township March 24, 1858, the son of Thomas and Jane Ralston, pioneer settlers in the Argyle area. He married Hannah McAffee of Roscoe Nov. 6, 1890, and they lived in Chicago ever since. He is survived by his wife; a daughter, Evelyn, at home; three sons, Thomas, Kenneth and William, all of Argyle; 12 grandchildren, and a sister, Mrs. Elizabeth McKay, Redwood Falls, Minn. A daughter, Dorothy, preceded him in death. Funeral services will be held in Chicago and also at Argyle, at 2:30 p.m. Friday in the chapel at the Scottish cemetery, where he will be buried.*" (Taken from a newspaper clipping).


Hannah Jane McAffee, daughter of James McAffee and Margaret Louise Cross, was born 10 March 1867 at their home in Roscoe. She attended and graduated from Roscoe Union High School. A picture of her sister Julia's high school class is on page 22 of "The Picture Story of Roscoe".

She took special training to become a teacher. She was a teacher at Bell School, and two others, one east of Roscoe. According to tradition, boys at the school east of Roscoe brought guns to school for target practice during recess on at least one occasion, supposedly it was the Lovesee boys. Their family was among pioneer Roscoe settlers.

Harlan V. Holt was her principal and her teacher in Roscoe, 1885 - 1886. (He later became a Methodist preacher and had a church in Avondale. This was why they moved there after first living near Lincoln Park following marriage.)

She married P. Wm. Ralston, son of Thomas Ralston and Jean Ralston, on 6 November 1890. The ceremony was at her parent's home on the property originally settled by Robert J. Cross. She was said to have been expecting to live on a farm but was soon living in Chicago where her husband became employed in civil engineering survey work. She returned to Roscoe to have her first child Thomas, in August 1892. They lived near Lincoln Park for a short time, and then Avondale, before building the home in Irving Park at 4328 Lowell Avenue, about 1897-8. She told about entertaining relatives who visited Chicago for the World's Columbian Exposition in 1893. She belonged to Irving Park Methodist Church, was interested in church activities, and was President of the Women's Foreign Missionary Society for many years. She was a member of Irving Park Women's Club.

Hannah died at her Chicago home 23 January 1950. Burial was in Argyle Cemetery.

*"Hannah McAffee Ralston, died yesterday at the Belmont hospital in Chicago. She was the widow of the late Peter W. Ralston.*

*"Mrs. Ralston was born March 10, 1867, in Roscoe the daughter of James and Margaret McAffee. She was the granddaughter of Robert J. Cross, the first settler of Roscoe Township. She married Peter W. Ralston, Nov. 6, 1890, in Roscoe and the couple then moved to Chicago, where they have lived since then.*

*"Surviving are a daughter, Evelyn, at home: three sons, Thomas, Kenneth and William, all of Argyle, 12 grandchildren and three great-grandchildren. Besides her husband, a daughter preceded her in death.*

*"Funeral services will be held Wednesday at 2:30 p.m. in the chapel of the Scottish cemetery at Argyle."* (Taken from a newspaper clipping).

They had five children:

- 1) Thomas James, born 29 August 1892 at Roscoe, Ill. He served in France during WW1. He married Mabelle

Greenlee 22 December 1921. He died 1 February 1989, Argyle. They had three children.

- 2) Kenneth McAffee, born 21 November 1895, Chicago, married Evelyn Belden 15 June 1922, died 9 Sept. 1991, Roscoe. They had seven children.
- 3) Evelyn Margaret, born 17 October 1899, Chicago, died 29 December 2010, Evanston, Illinois.
- 4) Dorothy Jean, born 18 February 1901, Chicago, died 31 March 1920, Chicago.
- 5) William John Charles, born 14 June 1910, Chicago, married Margaret Jeanette Greenlee 19 February 1938, died 24 November 1990, Rockford. They had three children.

## Thomas Ralston and Jane (Jean) Ralston-

Thomas Ralston

Jane (Jean) Ralston

Thomas, fifth child of Peter Ralston and Janette Brown, was born 21 August 1827 at Homeston, Campbeltown Parish, Argyleshire, Scotland. He emigrated with his parents, Peter and Janet, from Campbeltown, Scotland in 1840 to New York on the British Barque "Tay" and they went to live with Janet's brother, Alexander Brown in Cincinnati, Ohio, and then in 1843 to Argyle, Illinois on West Lane Road. He died on the farm near Roscoe, 19 May 1879, age 51, as a result of injuries received while he was administering medication to a horse.

On the 29 August 1853 he (age 26) purchased from Luther Brown of Ashtabula, Ohio, the farmland described as W½ NW¼ Section 10 Township 45 North Range 2 East. Containing 80 acres and recorded in Vol. 17, page 66 at the General Land Office at Washington, D.C. The price was $400.00. This property later contained the farm buildings on McDonald road in Harlem Township, Winnebago County, Illinois. Luther Brown had bought it from the Government in October 28, 1839.[8]

On 8 February 1854 he purchased from Paul and Abigail Torrey of Naples, Ontario County, New York, the farmland described as E½ SW¼ Section 3 Township 45 R 2E, containing 80 acres. The price was $1,000.00. Paul B. Torrey had bought it from the Government April 15, 1841.[9]

On 5 June 1869 he purchased from his father Peter Ralston farmland described as NW part of NE¼ of NE¼ Section 14 (looks like 19 but probably 14) Township 45, containing 7 acres more or less. The cost was $100.00.[10]

On 1 November 1870 he purchased from Jabez and Lydia Love the farmland described as NW¼ SE¼ Section 3 Township 45, containing 40 acres. The price was $1,200.60.[11]

On 17 March 1873 he purchased from Jabez Love and Milton Rhodes and their wives the farmland described as S½ W½ SW¼ Section 3 Township 45, containing 40 acres. The price was $1,600.00.[12]

The farm on McDonald Road then had a total of 240 acres.

When Thomas died he left his widow and 7 children with the farm (3 sons and 4 daughters).

Jean Ralston was also called Jane. (Parish birth records show Jean but some family records show Jane.) The daughter of John Ralston and Isabelle Greenlee, she was born 16 April 1835 in Aucharua farm, Southend, Kintyre, Scotland. She married her second cousin Thomas Ralston in Illinois, 1 April 1857. He died on the farm near Roscoe, 19 May 1879, at age 51. She died in Roscoe 23 April 1924 at age 89.

*"MRS. RALSTON SUMMONED AT ROSCOE HOME...*

*Resident Here Since April, 1850...*

*Roscoe, April 23...*

*Mrs. Jane Ralston, a resident of this vicinity since 1850, died at the home of her son John, two miles south of Roscoe, early today.*

*"Jane Ralston was born in Argyleshire, Scotland, April*

*16, 1835, and came to America with her parents when 15 years of age,* (Passenger on bark Charlotte Harrison arriving in New York from Greenock, Scotland on July 15, 1850), *settling at Argyle. Her marriage to Thomas Ralston was solemnized in 1857 and the young couple resided on a farm between Caledonia and Argyle for several years. Since the death of her husband in 1879, Mrs. Ralston made her home with her son John "One other son, P. W. Ralston resides in Chicago. In addition, she is survived by three daughters, Mrs. Nettie McNaughton, of Redwood Falls, Minn., Mrs. Lizzie McKay, Belleview, Minn., and Mrs. Martha White of Keytesville, Mo. The latter was a resident of Rockford for several years. One daughter and a son preceded the mother in death. Mrs. Ralston's death came unexpectedly. A week ago a number of her local friends joined with her in the observance of her 89th birthday. "Several grandchildren also survive her, two of whom, Kenneth and Thomas, sons of P. W. Ralston, have made their home with her for several years. "Funeral arrangements have not been completed. The Rev. Edgar Smith, of the Argyle Presbyterian Church, of which Mrs. Ralston had been an active member, will probably officiate at the obsequies. Burial will be at Argyle."*

They had seven children: Peter William, Janette B, Isabelle G, Martha, John T, Elizabeth H and Thomas C.

# Peter Ralston and Jannet/Janet Brown

Peter Ralston, also called Patrick, first child of Thomas Ralston and Margaret Picken, was born in Scotland at Brecklate, Southend Parish, June 1791. On 21 January 1820 he married, in Southend, Jannet Brown of Machrimore born 1802 in Scotland, daughter of Charles Brown and Elizabeth Ralston.

Peter and Janet traveled with six of their children from Campbeltown, Scotland in 1840 to New York on the ship "*British Barque Tay*" and went to live with her brother, Alexander Brown in Cincinnati, Ohio, and then went to Illinois in 1843.

He was a charter member and elder in the Willow Cheek Presbyterian Church, Argyle, Winnebago Co., Illinois, organized in 1844.

Peter, the father, died 8 April 1879 in Illinois. Family documents include a Letters of Administration designating his grandson, Peter W. Ralston as the estate administrator June 6th 1879. His wife Janet Brown died, in Illinois in 1845.

They had eleven children·

1) Elizabeth, born 20 Dec. 1820, Homeston, Southend, Scotland. She married William Fleming, 11 June 1840 in Campbeltown and remained in Scotland in 1840. Both died in N Ireland.
2) Child died as infant.
3) Margaret, born 26 April 1824, Homeston, Campbeltown, Scotland. She married John Picken, June 1849 in Illinois, died in Ill.
4) Helen, born 24 Feb. 1826, Homeston, Campbeltown, Scotland died as infant.
5) Thomas, born 30 Aug. 1827 Homeston, Campbeltown, Scotland, married Jean Ralston, 1 Apr. 1857, died 19 May 1879 with burial in the Argyle, Ill. cemetery.
6) Charles, christened 27 Dec. 1829 Homeston, Campbeltown, Scotland, married, Ella Jackson, Tennessee native and cousin of Stonewall Jackson in

1869, and died 1889 in Lawrence, Douglas Co., Kansas, burial in Oak Hill Cemetery.

7) Helen, born 24 July 1832, Campbeltown, Scotland, married David Andrew.
8) Janet, born 12 Sept. 1834, Campbeltown, Scotland, married Archie McEachran.
9) Peter, born 23 May 1837, Homeston, Campbeltown, Scotland, bachelor, died 1916 in Lawrence, Douglas Co., Kansas, burial in Oak Hill Cemetery.
10) William, born about 1842 in Ohio, died about 1853, buried Argyle cemetery, lot 392.
11) Jane, born 8 Nov. 1845, infant died 20 Nov. 1845, buried Argyle cemetery, lot 392.

THE KINTYRE ANTIQUARIAN and NATURAL HISTORY SOCIETY MAGAZINE
Issue Number 54 autumn 2003.

*When Jannet Brown and Peter Ralston emigrated, they left a daughter, Mrs. Elizabeth Fleming, at Campbeltown. Elizabeth and her husband wrote from Campbeltown, on 30 July 1850, that 'a great many able young men left Kintyre this summer'. They sent 'respects to all our Brothers and sisters and to all ants (sic) & uncles and all inquiring friends'. The implication is that they not only knew a good number of Kintyre people in the USA, but also that there were extended families and generations of their relatives in the USA. The Fleming's also mentioned relatives and friends, including the 'Granlees (sic) family', who were expected in the USA, and 'John Ralston and Duggale Kerrale', destined for Canada. (The last name is the colloquial form of Dugald McKerral.) One group who had emigrated 'for America this summer will be across the Atlantik (sic) by this time'.*

# John Ralston and Isabell Greenlee/s

John Ralston the son of Alexander Ralston and Janet Howie (Huie) was christened 5 November 1789 in Brecklate, Southend, Scotland. He married Isabelle(a) Greenlee(s) 19 March 1819. She was born 1796 in Scotland, daughter of George Greenlee(s) and Martha Wilson, of Machribeg. She was a sister of John Greenlee, the founder of the Scottish Settlement in Northern Illinois. It was this family who sheltered John Greenlee and helped him in his escape to the United States

They emigrated to U.S.A. in 1850, leaving Campbeltown for Greenock and Glasgow to take the ship *Charlotte Harrison*, under Captain MacKintyre. They left for New York on 6 June 1850 with two sons and six daughters.

During the voyage they passed through a severe storm and were ordered to stay below with closed hatches. They found New York was holding memorial services with flags at half-mast and the streets lined with soldiers because of President Zachary Taylor's death on July 9th.

John and his family settled on a farm on Quail Trap Rd. on the north side of the Argyle Settlement. (See map in later section.)

John died 14 February 1865, Isabelle died 14 February 1879 in Caledonia Township, Boone Co., Illinois.


Isabell Greenlee the daughter of George Greenlees and Martha Wilson, was born 29 June 1796 at Machribeg Farm, Southend, Kintyre, Scotland. She married John Ralston 19 March 1819.

She was a sister of John Greenlee, the founder of the Scottish Settlement in Northern Illinois. It was this family who sheltered John Greenlee and helped him in his escape to the United States.

John and Isabell had nine children-
1)  Alexander: born 15 Jan. 1820, at Newton, Southend Parish, Scotland; married Margaret McKerral of Brunericken 28 Dec. 1843 in Southend.
2)  Martha: born 16 Sept. 1822, Southend Village.

3) George: born 22 June 1825, Aucharua, Southend; married Margaret McPhail.
4) Janet: born 26 Jan. 1828, Achrua, Southend.
5) Mary: born 29 June 1830, Achrua Southend.
6) Isabella: born 13 Dec. 1832, Achrua, Southend.
7) Jean (Jane): born 16 Apr. 1835, Achrua Southend; married Thos. Ralston. They had seven children. The parish birth records give her name as Jean but family records show Jane.
8) Ann Helen: born 6 Jul. 1838, Achrua, Southend.
9) Elizabeth: born 13 Oct. 1843, Achrua, Southend

# James McAffee and Margaret Cross-

James McAffee, 1901

Margaret Louise Cross

James McAffee was the son of Alexander McAffee and Jane McCarty. Born in Bradford, Co. Penn., 18 August 1827, he died at Roscoe, Illinois, 30 March 1901 on the former Cross farm, (Sec. 29 & 32), on the road from Roscoe to Rockton.

He came with his parents to Roscoe in 1839. They had a brick home south of Roscoe at the west side of the intersection of McDonald Road and North Second Street.

Following his father's death, he carried on at the McAffee farm and married Almeda McCausland (date unknown). She was from Ridott, Illinois, a native of Canada, and the daughter of William McCausland. She died in 1856, leaving one daughter, Meda.

He, and his brother Edwin, was in the Civil War. He enlisted August of 1862 and received a medical discharge 7 January 1863. The discharge certificate reads: "*James McAffee, a Sergeant of Captain Elias Cosper's Company, (E) of the 74th. Illinois* Regiment of the United States *Volunteers Infantry* was enlisted by Capt. *J. B. Kew* of the... Regiment of.... at *Harlem,*

*Winnebago Co., Illinois,* on the *11th. day of August* 1862, to serve 3 years; he was born in the *U. S. of America,* is *thirty five* years of age, *five* feet *nine* inches high, *light* complexion, *blue* eyes, *Brown* hair, and by occupation when enlisted a *Farmer.* During the last two months said soldier has been unfit for duty *60* days. (Surgeon's diagnosis is written here but, difficult to read). Discharged this *seventh* day of *January* 1863, at *Bowling Green, Ky. M.D.Manson, Br'g. Gen'l,* Commanding the Post. (Words in *italics* are hand written on blank spaces in document.)

The following is from The *'Rockford Daily Register-Gazette'* *"Mr. McAffee still lives but is gradually fading". "War Veteran Mustered Out...Roscoe, Ill., Mar. 30...James McAffee, who has been lingering between life and death for some days past, breathed his last this morning. He served in the Civil War as a Private in Co. E, 74th. Illinois Volunteers and was a member of Nevius Post G.A.R. He is survived by his wife, one son and three daughters. Funeral services will be held Monday afternoon at 1:30 from the house and 2:00 from the Methodist Church."*

The following is from *'Portrait and Biographical Record of Winnebago and Boone Counties, Illinois'* Chicago, Ill., 1892, Biographical Publishing Co.:

*"James McAffee was originally from the Keystone State, born in Bradford County in August, 1827, and his father Alexander McAffee, was also a native of that State but was born in Northumberland County in 1798. The elder Mr. McAffee married Miss Jane McCarty, of Lycoming County Pa., born at Muncy in 1800, and one of thirteen children. The result of this union was nine children, four sons and five daughters, two of whom died in early childhood. Of the seven that grew to adult years, only four now survive, and they are Amanda, now Mrs. Henry A. Fahnestock, at Waverly, Iowa; Mary A., widow of Melvin J. Wood, resides in Roscoe, Ill.; Edwin, a farmer of Audubon County, Iowa, and our subject, who is the eldest of the family. The parents of these children came West from Pennsylvania in October 1838, made the journey with teams, and landed in Roscoe on the 31st. of January 1839. While on the way to this State, they were in Michigan, near South Bend, Ind., for a*

*short time, and the father and his brother John came on to Roscoe Township, where they bought a claim of four hundred acres one-half mile from the (then) village of Roscoe. They paid $440 for this tract, and, although fifteen acres had been cultivated, there was no house on it. They immediately erected a double log house and then returned for the family. Here the father passed the remainder of his days, dying of an abscess in March, 1852, when not quite fifty four years of age. His wife remained a widow and survived him twenty-six years, keeping the family together until about 1870, when she went to live with her daughter. About this time the old place was sold for $4,500. Mrs. McAffee died in March 1878, when about seventy-eight years of age, her death occurring in Iowa, where she was visiting her daughter.*

*"James McAffee, subject of this sketch, and his brother Edwin were volunteers in the Civil War. The former enlisted in the Seventy-fourth Illinois Infantry as a Sergeant, August 1862, and was discharged for disability in January of the following year. (He applied for Invalid Pension in 1899) He and his brothers and sisters were all fairly educated, and our subject, being a man of observation and study, has not allowed his ideas to rust out, but is well informed on all subjects and is thoroughly apace with the times. After the death of his father, he carried on the farm and was married to Miss Almeda McCausland, of Ridott, Ill., but a native of Canada. Her father was William McCausland. Mrs. Almeda McAffee passed away in 1856, leaving one daughter, Meda, who is a resident of Iowa at the present time. Mr. McAffee's second marriage was to Miss Margaret L. Cross, a native of Roscoe, born in that city (or rather town at the time) in 1839. Her father, Robert J. Cross, was a native of Newburgh, N. Y., but moved to near Detroit, Mich., in 1825 and thence to Coldwater in 1830. Five years later, he came to Roscoe, Ill., where he became a successful agriculturist. He was quite a prominent man in the county and held many positions of trust and honor. He was the first County Commissioner appointed in 1836 and was the first County Treasurer appointed by the County Commissioners, serving in that capacity for three years. In 1846, he was elected by the Whigs of Winnebago County to represent them in the General Assembly and in 1846*

*and 1847 he was a colleague of Judge Church to revise the State Constitution. He was a profound thinker, a deep reasoner, and one of the ablest men the county has ever had. He died in February 1873, when sixty-nine years of age, and was at that time a member of the General Assembly from Winnebago and Boone Counties. His wife and four children still survive him. One son, John, is in Kansas; Margaret L. became the wife of our subject; William Henry is a Congregational minister of California, and Lewis is a farmer of Iowa. The mother of these children was born July 21, 1812, and, although nearly eighty years of age, is as bright mentally as ever, but her physical condition is not of the best.*

*"Mr. and Mrs. McAffee have been farmers in this section nearly all their lives and settled on the present farm, consisting of one hundred and thirty-five acres, which formerly constituted the home place of Mr. Cross. Their union has been blessed by the birth of three children, two daughters and one son: Hannah J., now Mrs. P. W. Ralston, residing in Chicago, her husband being a civil engineer; Julia E., now Mrs. Ernest I. Worcester, of Chicago, her husband an architect, and James C., a civil engineer working on the Columbian Exposition grounds, Chicago. Mr. McAffee is virtually a retired farmer, although living on the farm, which he has rented out for a number of years. He was born and reared a Democrat, but since 1860 has affiliated with the Republican party, although he is free to vote for the best man always."*

There is an interesting story told about James during the early days of Roscoe. It seems that one of the first buildings used for a school and church had planks instead of stairs. *"It is said of James McAffee that on one occasion he rode a borrowed horse up the planks in the church, and it took all the available men in town to get the horse down."*

On March 22, 1866, James remarried to Margaret L. Cross. She was "born in the large log house, built on the bank of Rock River on R J Cross farm", (Composition Book records kept by Hannah J McAffee Ralston)ˌ 21 April 1839 in Roscoe, Illinois, daughter of Robert J. Cross and Hannah Benedict.

He died March 30, 1901 in Roscoe.

City Directories and Census data-

- In 1900 Margaret L McAffee was living with her husband James McAffee in Roscoe
- In 1902 Margaret L McAffee, widow of James, was living with her daughter Julia and son-in-law Ernest I Worcester at 2520 N 44th Ave. Chicago.
- In 1910 Margaret McAffee, widow of James, was living with her daughter Hannah J and son-in-law Peter Ralston at 4328 Lowell Ave, Chicago
- In 1911 Margaret McAffee, widow of James, was living with her daughter Hannah J and son-in-law Peter Ralston at 4328 Lowell Ave, Chicago

She died in Chicago 18 October 1918 at the home of her daughter, Mrs. P. W. Ralston after a week's illness with pneumonia.

At the time, her other daughter Julia E. Worcester was also living in Chicago, and her son James C. McAffee was living in Beloit, Wisconsin. Her cousin, Mrs. Samuel Norton was living in Rockford, Ill.

They had three children: Hannah Jane, Julia Ellen and James Caten.

# Alexander McAffee and Jane McCarty

(No picture)

Alexander McAffee

Jane McCarty

Alexander McAffee was born in Northumberland Co., Pennsylvania, 2 November 1798, son of James McAffee and Martha McMichael. He died 24 March 1852 at Roscoe, Illinois.

*"Alexander and Jane McCarty were among the early pioneers to the far West. In October 1838 they with their family of five children, migrated to Roscoe, Illinois, by wagon and horseback, stopping for a time with friends in Michigan, with whom they left their women-folk, while they themselves pushed on, and finally located claims on the banks of Rock River, about one mile from the village of Roscoe, in northern Illinois. Mr. McAffee paid $400 for his claim of 400 acres. Here they erected a double log-house, and returned for the women and children. Chicago, ninety miles distant, was they're only market, and their produce was hauled there, and goods for their use brought back, for many years, by wagon. Here they reared their family of nine children. Both Alexander McAffee and his brother John, who accompanied him, were prominent in the community and occupied positions of trust."*

He left Pennsylvania in October 1838 and arrived in Roscoe 31 January 1839 after a short stay in Michigan near South Bend, Indiana. (His sister Mary and husband John McMichael, had moved to Harris Prairie, about eight miles northeast of South Bend in 1832 or 1833 with their family of nine children.)

He and his brother, John, bought a claim of four hundred acres a half mile south of Roscoe at a cost of $440. Fifteen acres had been under cultivation but there was no house. They built a double log house and returned for the family. Later there was a brick hotel at the west side, near of the intersection of McDonald Road.

He was first Township Supervisor from Harlem Township in 1850.

He married Jane McCarty of Muncy, Penn., on 7 November 1825. She was the daughter of William McCarty and Mary Lloyd, and was born in Muncy, Lycoming Co., on 6 April 1800, one of thirteen children.

They had nine children, 4 sons and 5 daughters (2 children died in early childhood):

1) James born in Penn., 18 August 1827, first married Almeda McCausland who died 1855, one child, Almeda. He remarried Margaret L. Cross and lived on the Cross farm north west of Roscoe. Three children, Hannah Jane, Julia Ellen, James Caten.

2) William D., born in Penn., 10 July 1829 .[4] A bachelor, died Roscoe 7 October 1862.

3) Amanda born in Penn., 28 February 1831 married Henry A. Fahnestock and lived in Waverly, Iowa. She died 4 January 1917, no children.

4) Ben Franklin, born Towanda 6 December 1832, died Towanda, 27 November 1834.

5) Charlotte Temple, born Towanda, 29 January 1836, died 17 February 1839, Roscoe, age 3.

6) Mary Ann, born Towanda., 16 January 1838 married Melvin J. Wood 1858 and lived in Roscoe. She died 22 February 1920, he 24 January 1890, no children.

7) Martha Jane, born in Roscoe, Ill., 8 June 1840, married Gust A. Wood, September 1870. One child Mabel born 30 December 1871, she married George Lovell.

8) Harriet born in Ill., 16 June 1842, married Ben F. Campbell had 2 children Alta and Fred. Harriet died 3 September 1888.

9) Edwin born in Ill., 8 June 1845, married Helen York of Byron, Illinois. He farmed in Audubon Co., Iowa. 4 children, Willis Herbert, Leslie Alexander, Edna Jane, and Elma, all born Exira, Iowa.

The following is taken from "Portrait and Biographical Record of Winnebago and Boone Counties, Illinois" Chicago, Ill., 1892, Biographical Publishing Co- *"James McAffee was originally from the Keystone State, born in Bradford County in August, 1827. His father Alexander McAffee was also a native of that State but was born in Northumberland County in 1798. The elder Mr. McAffee married Miss Jane McCarty, of Lycoming County Pa., born at Muncy in 1800, and one of thirteen children. The result of this union was nine children, four sons and five daughters, two of whom died in early childhood. Of the seven that grew to adult years, only four now survive, and they are Amanda, now Mrs. Henry A. Fahnestock, at Waverly, Iowa; Mary A., widow of Melvin J. Wood, resides in Roscoe, Ill.; Edwin, a farmer of Audubon County, Iowa, and our subject who is the eldest of the family. The parents of these children came West from Pennsylvania in October, 1838, made the journey with teams, and landed in Roscoe on the 31st. of January, 1839. While on the way to this State, they were in Michigan, near South Bend, Ind., for a short time, and the father and his brother John came on to Roscoe Township, where they bought a claim of four hundred acres one-half mile from the (then) village of Roscoe. They paid $440 for this tract, and, although fifteen acres had been cultivated, there was no house on it. They immediately erected a double log house and then returned for the family."*
*"Alex and his Brother John stayed with Jenks family while building it. Alex built the brick farm house about a mile south of the village about 1849 with James the son helping to haul the brick from Milwaukee at age 21. After the marriage of children, the farm was sold to Theo. Malott. It was an early day tavern on the main road north from Rockford. Alex's brother John built a house across the road further south, a short distance north of Lovejoy School."*

*"Here the father passed the remainder of his days, dying of an abscess in March, 1852, when not quite fifty four years of age. His wife remained a widow and survived him twenty-six years,*

*keeping the family together until about 1870, when she went to live with her daughter. About this time the old place was sold for $4,500. Mrs. McAffee died in March, 1878, when about seventy-eight years of age, her death occurring in Iowa, where she was visiting her daughter."*

Jane McCarty, daughter of William McCarty and Mary Lloyd, was born on 6 April 1800 in Muncy, Lycoming Co., Pa. Following Alec's death, Jane lived on at the Roscoe farm until about 1870, when it was sold for $4,500 and she went to live with a daughter, Amanda, in Iowa. She died there in Waverly 9 March 1878 and was buried in Roscoe, Winnebago Co., Illinois.

# Robert Cross and Hannah Benedict

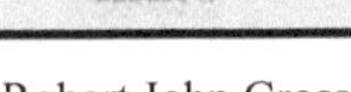

Robert John Cross

Hannah/*Susannah* Benedict Cross

Robert John Cross was born 1 October 1803 in Newburgh, Orange County, New York. He was the son of Rev. John Cross and Margaret Hanna Cross. Robert died 15 February 1873 in Roscoe, Winnebago Co., IL

"During his years of minority Robert resided mostly in Bethel, Sullivan Co., of that state."

Report of the Pioneer Society of the State of Michigan, vol. 2, 1901, an article by Judge Wm. H. Cross: "In the month of June, 1825, just one year from the time of the first settlement of Tecumseh, now fifty-four years ago, my brother, Robert J. Cross, entered four hundred acres of land on section eight. Before making this selection he had been through the south part of Oakland County the northwest part of Wayne County, and all the settlements of Washtenaw County, and finally made choice of a farm in Tecumseh. "On the last day of September, 1826, we came to Tecumseh to make it our home. On Sunday morning, the first day of October, we started up the river on the west side to find our land. We passed Jacob Woodward's ...etc."

"During that fall and winter (1826), we built our log cabin, and for more than a year and a half it was the extreme cabin of the settlement on the east side of the river, and on the main trail up and down the river, and at least a score of Indians passed our place to one white man..." (He goes on to describe other experiences.)

"In the autumn of 1827, my brother and myself were taken down with the fever and ague, and on writing back to our mother that we were ill, she determined to come and see her sick boys; and in November of that year she came and kept house for us--we having kept bachelor's hall till then. But when winter was over it was the wish of our mother to go to Tecumseh on the Sabbaths to attend meeting, for once in six, then four, and ere long, two weeks we had preaching, and I being the youngest must provide a way to go. So, on Sunday morning I must start out and find the oxen and yoke them to the large lumber wagon; then get mother into the wagon, and start for the school house, which was also the meeting house, and by the time we reached Brownville, we would have a wagon load of women and children, and the men were walking alongside. On arriving at the school house we would chain the oxen to a wheel of the wagon, seat ourselves on the slab benches, and perhaps worship as fervently and acceptably as cushioned pews to rest in, and a hired choir to sing our songs of praise for us. After the service we used to ride home leisurely in the strong carriage, and get home before night.... etc."

"In 1829 I took a trip on White Pigeon and Mottsville to haul a load of goods to Mr. Taylor, an Indian trader, located at the Chicago trail and the St. Joseph river, and then I first saw a western prairie, but while the trip was a rough and tedious one, the country so pleased me that my brother and I sold our farms the next year, and in the autumn of 1830 we bought land, and removed to Coldwater in Branch county, only returning to Tecumseh in 1832 to take to my new home the girl who had agreed to share life with me in the pioneer's cabin." (There are about four printed pages of this account, but no more mention of his brother, Robert J. Cross who went to Roscoe area in 1835. I guess their mother came back to Michigan again since the Coldwater history shows she had 80 acres there in 1834 and 162 acres in 1836. Supposedly she died there in 1846 at Ann Arbor.)

From History of Branch Co., Mich., 1879; "Col. A. F. Bolton was the first justice of peace for Coldwater, receiving his appointment in the fall of 1830; Robert J. Cross being the second, of whom it is related that on being proposed for the office he at first declined, but on being pressed accepted on condition that one of his friends, better versed in judicial lore, teach him the difference between a summons and a subpoena..."

"The following entries were made on ground covered by the township: Margaret Cross, 162.73 acres, March 28, 1836; Wm. H. Cross, 40 acres, Oct. 22, 1835; Wm. H. Cross 146.16 acres, Oct. 22, 1835; Margaret Cross, 80 acres, May 15, 1834, Wm. H. Cross, 80 acres, Aug. 27, 1831; Wm. H. Cross, 53.15 acres, Jan. 6, 1836."

The following is a quotation. "When about 22 years of age, he with a younger brother, decided to emigrate to the then far West, and going to Detroit, purchased a farm in Tecumseh, Lenawa Co., where he remained until 1830. He and his brother then sold out and removed to Coldwater, Mich., where they remained until June, 1835, when he came to his present residence in Winnebago Co., Illinois, (where he continually resided until his death). The next year he married Miss Hannah Benedict, of Monroe Co., N. Y., who still survives him. (She was a charter member of the Roscoe Congregational Church organised 28 November 1843.)

At the time Mr. Cross came to Roscoe, no land was in market and he was forced to purchase a squatter's right to his present farm, and as some of the land in Wisconsin was subject to entry in the Green Bay land district, he selected some along the Rock River from Janesville to Beloit, and on foot and alone he made his way to Green Bay, through an unbroken wilderness, and bought his land in Wisconsin.

From thence via the lakes he returned to Detroit and Coldwater, and in the fall of that year became the occupant of the present homestead. Mr. Cross was essentially a pioneer--a man of strong frame of body, of unyielding tenacity for the right; even in boyhood the champion of the feeble, or those he deemed oppressed.

"He was a stalwart oak, on whom could ever lean the feeble and the frail--as Minister E. B. Washburne declared, a "Noble Old Roman." A farmer all his life, and yet a firm, reliable business man, as a life constantly occupied in public affairs proved him to be. Yet he was ever as tender in heart as a little child, and his sympathy was even larger than his frame, or his purse; and truly was it said of him, those who knew him best, loved him most.

"During his residence of 36 years in this County, Mr. Cross was closely and intimately identified with its development, politically, socially and materially, never being backward in anything that would aid in its moral or religious advancement. A warm friend of education, he always lent a willing hand to aid in building school houses and establishing schools.

"Mr. Cross assisted at the organization of the county, being a member of the election board for the first election ever held in it, August, 1836. He was elected by the County Commissioners in 1836, at their first meeting, County Treasurer, which position he held for three years. In 1846, he was elected by the Whigs as a representative to the General Assembly for his county, and in 1847, by them as the colleague of Hon. Selden M. Church, a delegate to revise the Constitution of the State. In 1862, he was an independent candidate for the position of delegate to the Convention to again revise the constitution, but was defeated by a small plurality. In 1869 he was unanimously nominated by the Republicans for member of the Convention that formed our present constitution, and was elected without opposition. Later he was nominated by the Republicans and elected one of the three members from Winnebago and Boone Counties to the General Assembly. In all these legislative bodies he has borne an honorable and conspicuous part.

"In addition to this, Mr. Cross was Chairman of the Board of Supervisors several years, occupying that position at the time of his death.

"He was also township School Fund Trustee for over thirty consecutive years, during which time the township never suffered loss from the funds being loaned on insufficient securities, as was the case in most townships.

"He had five children, John, Margaret, Louisa, William Henry, Marie Antoinette (deceased), and Lewis. The estimation in which he was held was manifest by delegations of early settlers of the county, members of the Board of Supervisors and from the State Legislature, in attendance at his funeral."

"The first claims against the county were presented at this session, (August 1836). Germanicus Kent, Robert J. Cross and J. P. Griggs, as judges of election, and D. A. Spaulding and S. A. Lee, as clerks, were allowed one dollar each...D. A. Spaulding was allowed fifty cents for stationery furnished for poll-books."

"At that time the assessment was made by the county treasurer, and taxes were collected by the Sheriff. R. C. Cross, the treasurer, consumed fifteen days in making this assessment. His compensation was thirty dollars, or two dollars per day. He was also allowed nine dollars and twenty-eight cents, for receiving and disbursing the taxes when collected. This commission was two per cent on four hundred and sixty-four dollars, the amount actually collected."

The Winnebago County Agricultural Society "was organized April 13, 1841. Dr. Haskell was elected president; Robert J. Cross, vice-president. An exhibition was held on the 13th. of October. Thus was held, in a single day, the first cattle show in northern Illinois."

"In pursuance of an act of the general assembly, approved February 20, 1847, a constitutional convention assembled at Springfield, June 7th of the same year. The delegates from Winnebago County were Selden M. Church and Robert J. Cross... Upon organization of the convention, Mr. Church was appointed a member of the standing committee on the organization of departments and office connected with the executive department; Mr. Cross, a member of the committee on the bill of rights... On June 26th. Mr. Cross introduced the following resolution: 'Resolved, That the committee on elections and the right of suffrage be instructed to inquire into the expediency of changing the time of holding elections from the first Monday in August to the Tuesday next after the first Monday in November, and the manner of voting from 'vive voce' to ballot.' Mr. Cross also led in an effort to secure the new constitution a provision for a state superintendent of schools, with a liberal salary."

Hannah (AKA Susannah) BENEDICT was born on 21 July 1812 in Nassau, Rensselaer, NY, first child of Jacob Benedict and Rhoda Beebe. She died on 4 Oct. 1893 in Roscoe, Winnebago Co., IL

Hannah BENEDICT and Robert John CROSS were married on 18 Sep. 1836 in Nassau, Rensselaer, NY, (or, in Perington, Monroe, NY).

They had five children: John, Margaret L, William H, Mary A and Lewis B.

# Kenneth Ralston and Evelyn Belden-Cousins

**They are descended from John Belding.
Their 6th great grandfather.**

| | |
|---|---|
| **1. Kenneth (1895-1991) is the son of Hannah Jane McAffee** | **1. Evelyn (1902-1985) is the daughter of Louis Andrew Belden** |
| **2. Hannah (1867-1950) is the daughter of Margaret Louise (Cross) McAffee** | **2. Louis (1874-1938) is the son of Allen H Belden** |
| **3. Margaret (1839-1918) is the daughter of Hannah** | **3. Allen (1849-1916) is the son of Philo Belden** |
| **4. Hannah (1812-1893) is the daughter of Rhoda (Beebe) Benedict** | **4. Philo (1815-1889) is the son of Jonathan Belden** |
| **5. Rhoda (1788-1832) is the daughter of Miriam (Kellogg) Beebe** | **5. Jonathan (1778-1831) is the son of Jonathan Belden** |
| **6. Miriam (1755-?) is the daughter of Silas Kellogg** | **6. Jonathan (1737-1778) is the son of Silas Belden** |
| **7. Silas (1714-1792) is the son of Lydia (Belden) Kellogg** | **7. Silas (1691-1742) is the son of Jonathan Belden** |
| **8. Lydia (1675-1759) is the daughter of John Belding I** | **8. Jonathan (1660-1734) is the son of John Belding I** |
| **9. John (1635-1677) the sixth great grandfather of Kenneth.** | **9. John (1635-1677) the sixth great grandfather of Evelyn.** |

John Belding/Belden, son of Richard Belden and Margaret Ackrendon, was born in the Parish of Heptonstall, West

Yorkshire, England, baptized 8 February 1634 (18 February 1635 N.S.) as John "Baldon", and accompanied his father to America, settling in Wethersfield, where he was made a freeman in 1657.

He was licensed to be a tavern keeper by the town, and in all probability was a merchant.

John Belden married Lydia 24 April 1656 (4 May 1656 N.S.), who might have been Lydia Standish, daughter of Thomas and Susanna Standish, or Lydia Ryley.

He died June 27, 1677, aged forty-six years. The inventory of his estate, taken by James Treat, John Deming and Samuel Wright, amounted to 911 pounds. Legatees were his children John, Jonathan, Joseph, Samuel, Daniel, Ebenezer, Sarah, Lydia and Margaret (who was just 5 months old).

# Pictures-

Mom, Russell, Harold, Larry, and Dad, about 1928

Harold, Laurence, Dad, and Russell at Chicago home of Grandfather Peter W Ralston

Harold, Laurence, and Russell at farmhouse front steps, about 1929,
wearing clothes made by Grandmother Hannah J Ralston

Laurence, Harold and Russell at back door of Ralston farm home, Roscoe,
Illinois

Russell, Harold, Laurence with Dad beside 1927 Chevrolet in Roscoe farm driveway

Harold, Dad, Laurence, and Russell

**Laurence, Russell, Harold**

Evelyn B. Ralston and 4 sons; Laurence, David, Harold and Russell Ralston

**Laurence and David Ralston, about 1933**

**Russell, Laurence, David, Dad and Harold with watermelons**

**Russell, Laurence and Harold on way to school**

**Harold, David, Russell, and Laurence with teacher, carrying lunch bags**

**Dad, Russell, David, Laurence and Harold, about 1933**

**Harold, Mary Jane, Laurence and David**

Laurence, David and Harold with baseball gloves, wearing 4H club team shirts

Harold Laurence Russell and David with baseball equipment in backyard of Roscoe farm

**David, Harold, Russell and Laurence with 4-H club lambs**

**Laurence, Harold, Russell and Dad at back of house, Ralston farm, Roscoe, Illinois**

Dad, Duane, Mom, Mary Jane, Harold, Laurence, Russell and David
Ralston

Evelyn B and Kenneth M Ralston, 40th wedding anniversary

Ralston families at Uncle Tom Ralston's farm in Argyle, Illinois, about 1939

Ralston family in Chicago about 1940 Front- Mary Jane; Next- Harold,
Peter W, Hannah J, David, Philip; Next- Russell, Laurence, Evelyn M, William J,
Mabelle, Wallace, Thomas J, Kenneth, Evelyn B, Duane, Carolyn

Peter W Ralston home, Chicago, Illinois; about 1898

**1883 Hannah J McAffee**

Hannah Jane McAffee

**Hannah J, Thomas J, and Peter Wm Ralston, February 1895**

Kenneth McAffee Ralston, March 13, 1915

Kenneth McAffee Ralston

Dorothy Jean (1901-1920) and Evelyn Margaret Ralston (1899-2010)

Evelyn M and Dorothy Ralston; about 1910

Grandma Hannah Ralston, Earl and Esther Worcester, and children (Thelma,and Robert?) Ralston Farm, Roscoe, Illinois

**Earl James Worcester family, (1st cousin once removed)**

**Back- Evelyn M, Kenneth, Hannah J, Peter W and Dorothy; Front- William and Jane Ralston; about 1918**

Front- Dorothy, Evelyn; Back- Peter W, Kenneth, Thomas J and Hannah J Ralston; about 1908

50th Anniversary of Peter W and Hannah J Ralston, 1940

Front- Kenneth McAffee Ralston, Archibald McKay; Next- Hannah McAffee Ralston, Martha Ralston White, Elizabeth Ralston McKay, Thomas J Ralston; Back- Peter W Ralston, John T Ralston, Janette Ralston McNaughton, Jane Ralston, Jean McKay, Isabelle Ralston Smith; Rear portrait- Thomas Ralston; center portrait- Thomas C Ralston; about 1898

1898 Ralston homestead: Jane, Isabelle, John Ralston and hired man

Front- Peter Wm, Jeanette B, John T; Back- Thomas C (obscure), Martha, Isabelle G, Elizabeth; Ralston Siblings about 1885

Front- Hannah J, William J, Peter W; Back- Dorothy, Evelyn, Kenneth and
Thomas J Ralston; about 1914

Kenneth Ralston and "Aunt Nettie McNaughton"; she would be Grandpa
Peter Ralston's sister Janette; about 1920

Aunt "Nettie" Ralston McNaughton and Kenneth Ralston

Great Grandmother Jane Ralston and daughters about 1890. Possibly
Elizabeth (1873-1949) and Isabelle (1863-1919)

front- Jeane Ralston, Molly Ralston, Isabella Ralston, Elizabeth Ralston.
middle- Martha Ralston,# 2, John R McDonald,# 4,# 5, Peter Ralston.
rear- #1, Isabelle McDonald, John Mcdonald, Isabelle G Ralston, John T Ralston.
As Identified by Kenneth McAffee Ralston about 1990.
All descendants of John Ralston and Isabelle Greenlee. About 1885-1890

**Descendants of 2nd Great Grandfather John Ralston, about 1890**

Great Grandmother Jane Ralston

Unknown person

**Front- Jane; Back- Thomas, Wallace and Peter W Ralston; 1922**

**Thomas, Wallace, Jane, Peter Ralston; 4 generations, 1922**

**Thomas and Kenneth Ralston about 1896**

**Kenneth, Evelyn M, Dorothy and Thomas J Ralston; about 1905**

**Left- Kenneth and Thomas Ralston; Right- Cousins Jean and Archie McKay**

Evelyn M Ralston; about 1900

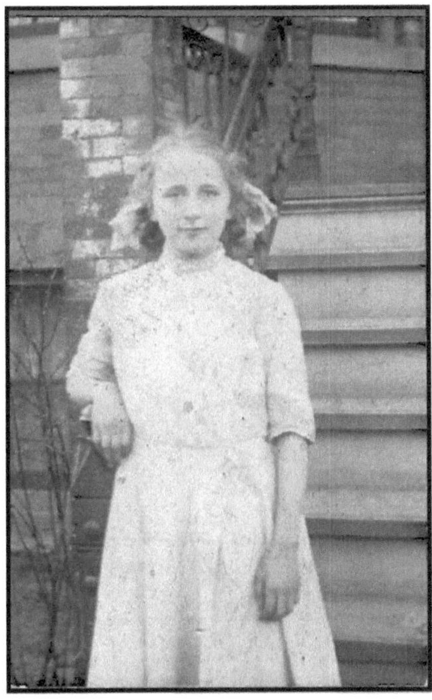

Dorothy Jean Ralston

**Evelyn M Ralston**

**Grandparents Peter W and Hannah J Ralston; about 1942**

Kenneth McA. Ralston, George McDonald (?), Thomas J Ralston; about
1920

Evelyn M and Kenneth McA. Ralston, about 1920

Kenneth, Evelyn M and Thomas Ralston, siblings, about 1920

**Kenneth and William Ralston**

**Fun on the Farm; Evelyn M Ralston at right front, some others from neighboring McDonald family**

**Aunt Evelyn M Ralston**

**Thomas, Evelyn M and Kenneth Ralston**

Left-?, Evelyn M Ralston, ?, Evelyn B Ralston, ?

Madelyn Worcester (Lennartson), unknown, Grace McDonald (Barnes) and
Evelyn M Ralston

**Unknown, Evelyn M Ralston, Madelyn Worcester, and Dorothy Jean Ralston**

**Dorothy J Ralston, cousin Madelyn Worcester and Evelyn M Ralston**

**Evelyn M Ralston and Grace I McDonald**

**2nd cousins; Fred and Wayne Worcester**

**Jean White Fitch and Dorothy J Ralston**

**Evelyn M Ralston, cousin Madelyn Worcester and Grace McDonald**

Evelyn M Ralston and Grace McDonald

?, ?, Evelyn M Ralston, Florence McDonald, ?, Blanche McDonald

**Group with 2nd left, Evelyn M Ralston**

**1st- George McDonald, Grace McDonald, Welcome Andrew, Laura Greenlee, Lillian Andrew, Florence McDonald? 2nd- Kenneth M Ralston, Florence?, Lewis Greenlee, ? Andrew, ?, Ralph Barnes, Beth Andrew, Thomas Ralston. 3rd- John McDonald, Dorothy J Ralston, Mary McDonald, Jean E White, Mabelle Greenlee, George Barnes, Francis Picken?, Blanche McDonald, Evelyn M Ralston, Isabelle McDonald**

Eleanor Brown Ralston, Florence McEachran Williams, Ruby McEachran Picken, Ruth McCathran Andrew and Maude Brown Rogers

Mary, Isabelle, Grace, Mary, and Blanche McDonald

**Vida McNaughton, 1st cousin once removed**

**Grandmother Hannah J and Aunt Evelyn M Ralston; about 1949**

**2nd Great Grandfather Robert J Cross and siblings- William Hanna and Margaret; about 1845**

**Hannah Benedict Cross and son William**

**Jacob Benedict (1779 – 1855), father of Hannah Benedict Cross (courtesy of Connie Ralston Kassal)**

**Written on the reverse- "Towanda, PA : home of John McAffee; father of Margaret, grandmother of Jim. Also Alexander and Wm. brothers of John. Alex, father of James; father of Meda, Hannah, Julia, James C. (The brothers came to Harlem Twp. January 1839)**

James McAffee; about 1900

James McAffee

**James McAffee and Margaret Cross McAffee**

**Adeline Alden McAffee (1816-1891) , wife of 2nd Great Granduncle, John McAffee**

"Kitty Irvine", 1st Cousin 3 times removed

Henry Augustus (Gust) Fahnestock (1833/5-1920);

1st cousin 3 times removed, married to Amanda McAffee (1831-1917)

Unidentified, 3rd from back left is probably Henry White (he married Peter W Ralston's sister, Martha).

Lovejoy School 1870

**Brecklate farm home, Kintyre, Scotland-**

**Birthplace of 2nd Great Grandfather Peter Ralston in 1791**

**Aucharua Farm, Kintyre Scotland-**

**Birthplace of Great Grandmother Jane Ralston in 1835**

# Kenneth McAffee Ralston sketches- about 1914

# Farm Scenes-

**Three-horse team in harness, K Ralston farm, Roscoe, Illinois**

**Prize Bull**

**Cattle at feed bunk, Kenneth Ralston farm, Roscoe, Illinois**

**Cattle in pasture, Kenneth Ralston farm, Roscoe, Illinois**

**Cattle in barnyard waiting for feed wagon, chickens looking for grain, Kenneth Ralston farm, Roscoe, Illinois**

**Cattle at feeders, Kenneth Ralston farm, Roscoe, Illinois**

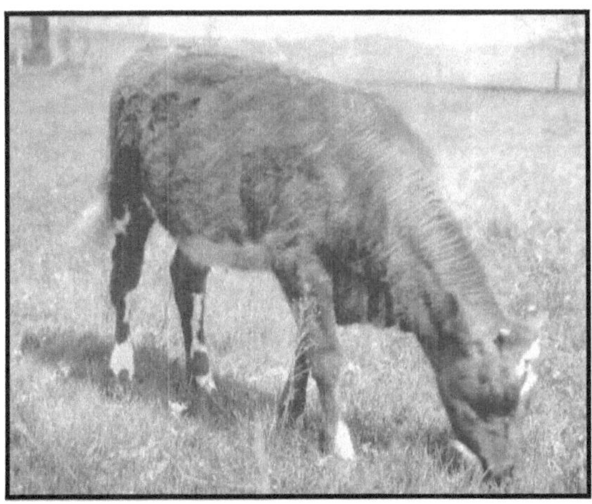

**Feeding on pasture**

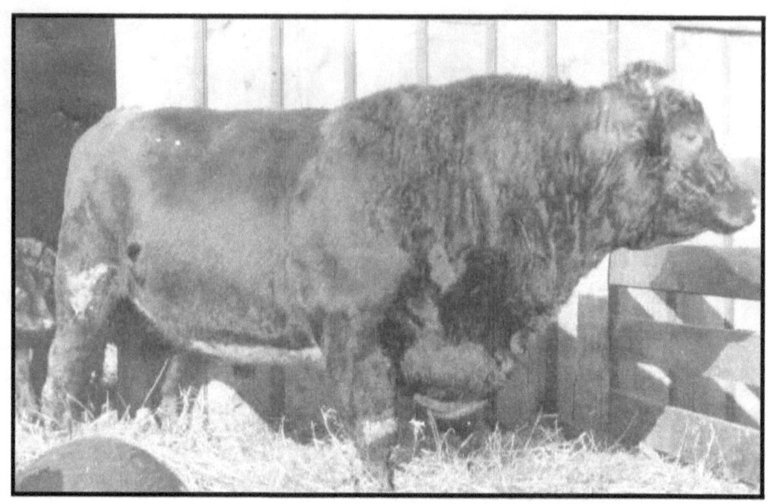

**Fat Steer, Kenneth Ralston farm, Roscoe, Illinois**

**Cattle in barnyard, Kenneth Ralston farm, Roscoe, Illinois; about 1922**

**Ralston farmhouse, Roscoe, Illinois, about 1930**

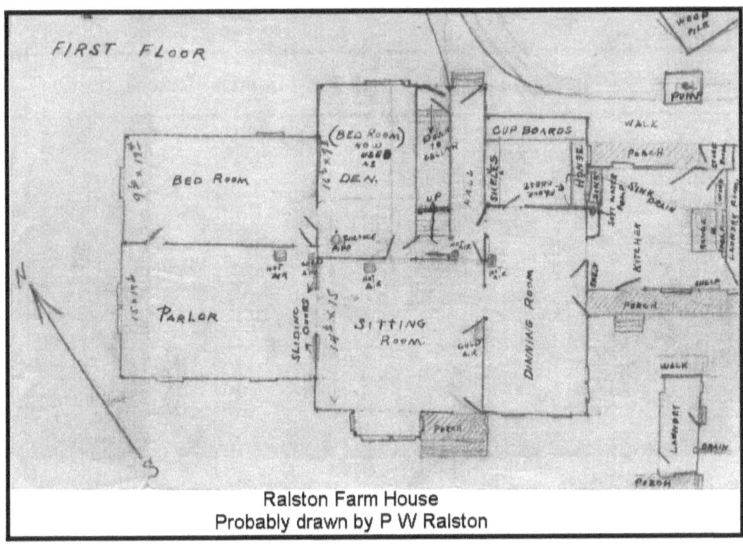


Ralston Farm House
Probably drawn by P W Ralston

**Floor plan of Ralston farm home, Roscoe, Illinois**

**Farm buildings, Kenneth Ralston farm, Roscoe, Illinois**

**Ralston farm buildings, Roscoe, Illinois, about 1930**

**Childhood Home of Great Grandmother Jane Ralston  (Sketch about 1890)**

Roscoe, Illinois parade by Methodist Church

Harlem High School, corner of N. Second St. and Harlem Road

**Hogs in barnyard, Kenneth Ralston farm, Roscoe, Illinois**

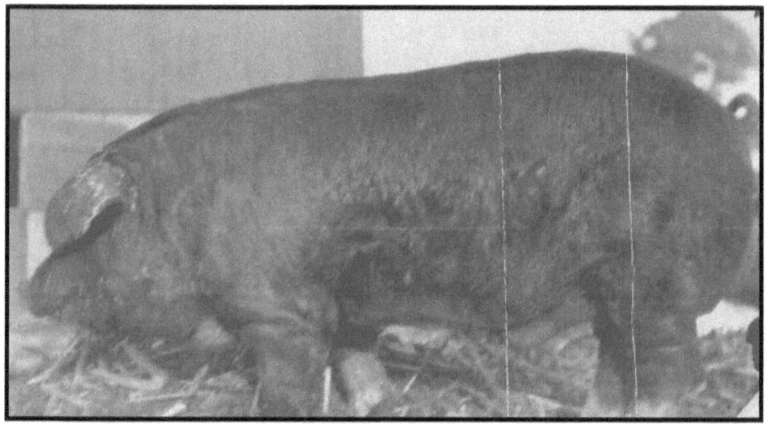

**Hog in barnyard, Kenneth Ralston farm, Roscoe, Illinois**

**Horses harnessed to corn cultivator in field, Kenneth Ralston farm, Roscoe, Illinois**

**Four-horse team harnessed to plow, Kenneth Ralston farm, Roscoe, Illinois**

Horses and manure spreader in barnyard, Thomas Ralston farm, Roscoe, Illinois

Kenneth M Ralston, March 1923

**Sheep at feeders and in pasture, Kenneth Ralston farm, Roscoe**

**April 17, 1921; big snow in front of hog house; K Ralston farm, Roscoe**

# Documents-

Assessed *Taxes.*—Notice of Assessment for the Year 1829, ending at Whitsunday 1830.

To *Thos Ralston*

TAKE NOTICE, That by virtue of the Acts of Parliament for granting the several Duties under-mentioned, you are charged in my District as under.—Witness my Hand, this 25

day of *July* 18—

⎱ Surveyor.
⎰ Residence.

House and Window Duty, as per Notice formerly given   -   -   £

*Note.—The Duty on all the following Articles is charged according to the Number kept, &c. from Whitsunday 1828 to Whitsunday 1829*

Duty on Male Servants, viz.

Four Wheel Carriages

Two Wheel Carriages

Horses used for riding or drawing Carriages

Other Horses and Mules

Dogs

Hair Powder

Armorial Bearings

Horse Dealers

Which several Duties must be paid to the Collector thereof at his Office on or before the 25th day of *March* next, in terms of the statutes.

If you consider yourself aggrieved by the above Charges, or any of them, you are hereby required to give me Notice in Writing within FIFTEEN DAYS after the date hereof, stating the particular wrong or grievance of which you complain; without which Notice, within the time aforesaid, no Appeal will be received. The day and place of hearing Appeals may be learned, by applying to me, or to the Collector.

**1830 Tax Assessment for 1829; 3rd Great Grandfather (1759-1833) Thos Ralston, Scotland**

*Hamilton County, Treasurer's Office,* 184/

RECEIVED of *Peter Ralston* the sum of Dollars Cents Mills, being in full of the Tax assessed for State, County, Jail, Township, Road, Bridge, and School purposes, for the year 184/ on the following property:

| Range. | Town. | Sec. | Acres. | VALUE. $ | TAX. $ |
|--------|-------|------|--------|----------|--------|

*Hamilton County, Treasurer's Office,* 184

RECEIVED of the sum of Dollars Cents Mills, being in full of the Tax assessed for State, County, Jail, Township, Road, Bridge, and School purposes, for the year 184 on the following property:

| Range. | Town. | Sec. | Acres. | VALUE. $ | TAX. $ |
|--------|-------|------|--------|----------|--------|

**2nd Great Grandfather Peter Ralston Tax payment receipts, Hamilton, Co., OH; 1841 & 42. For $64.00 and $74.42**

Church letter reference of 2<sup>nd</sup> Great Grandparents Peter Ralston, and Jannet Brown Ralston and Great Grandaunt Margaret Ralston;  from 5th Presbyterian Church, Cincinnati, OH to a church in Illinois; April 7, 1843

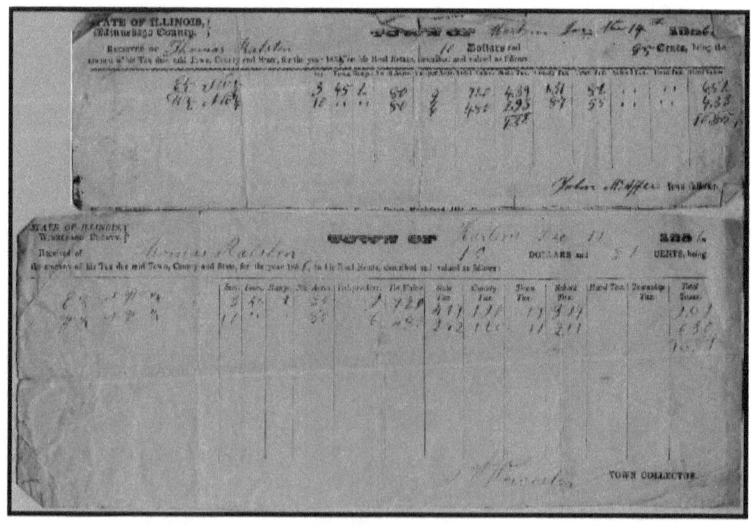

1856 Tax bill, Thomas Ralston, Harlem Township, Winnebago County, Illinois

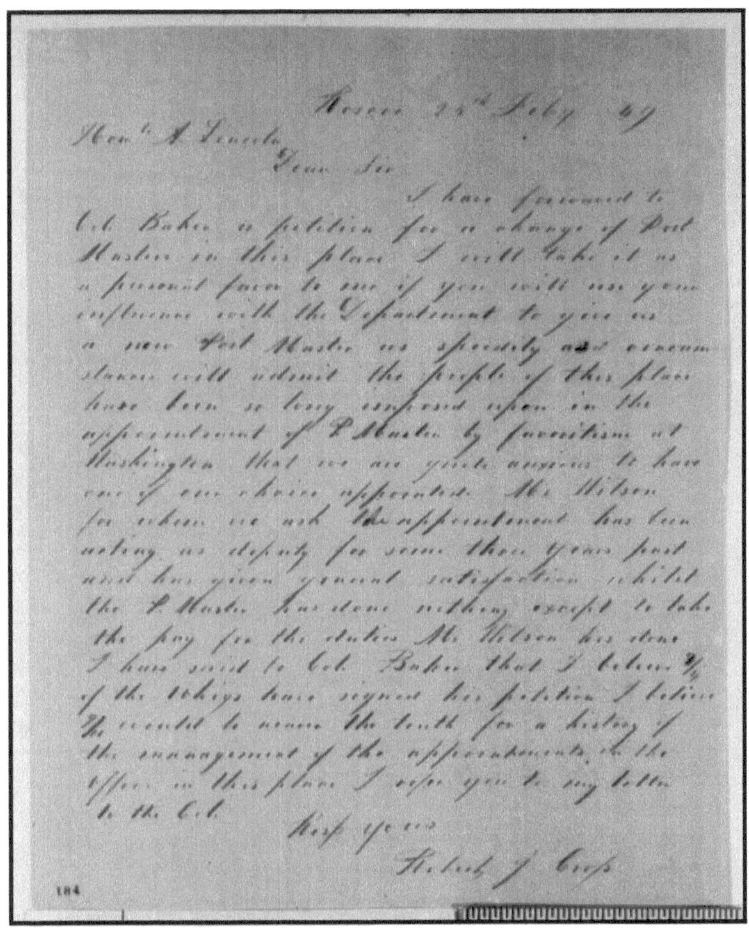

**Letter from 2nd Great Grandfather Robert J Cross to President Lincoln, July 1864; requesting Roscoe, Illinois Postmaster replacement**

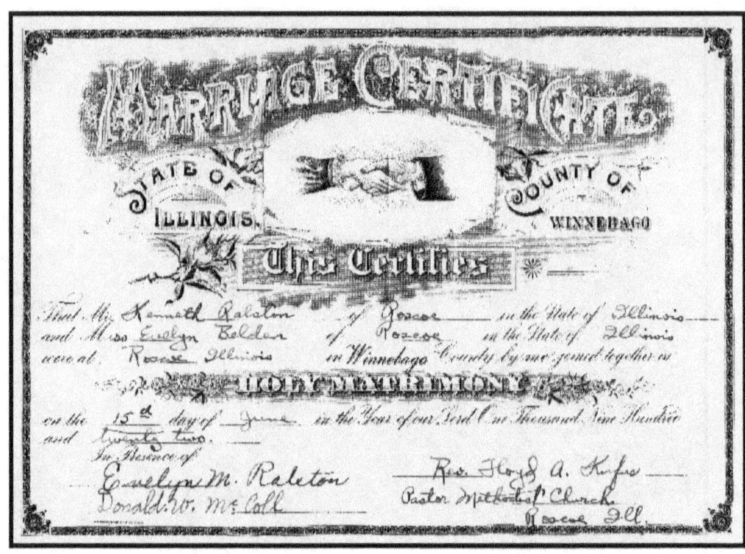

**Marriage Certificate, Kenneth and Evelyn B Ralston, June 15, 1922, Roscoe, Illinois**

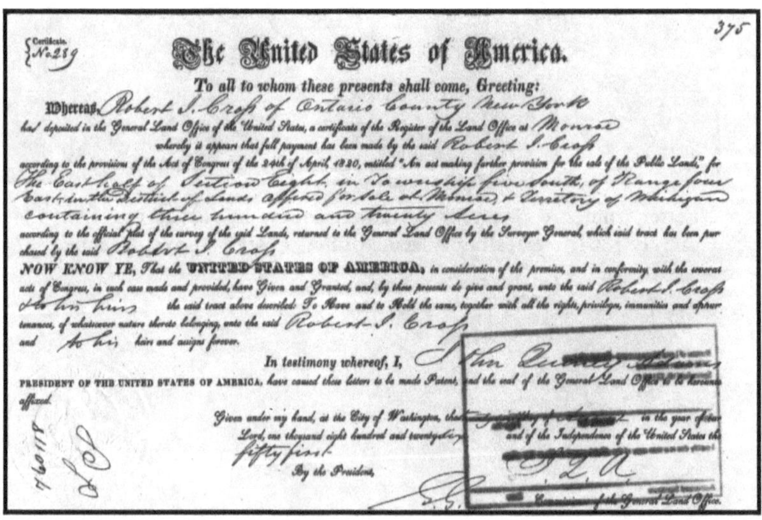

**1826 Land Patent, Robert J Cross in Monroe, Territory of Michigan**

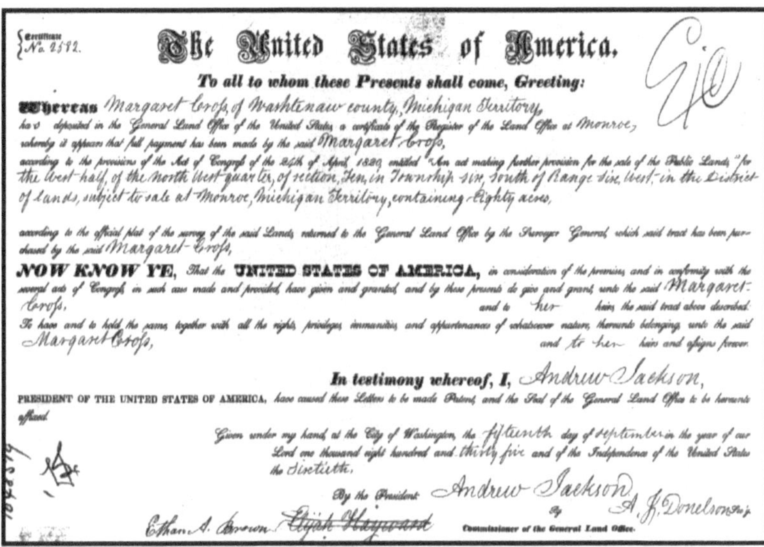

1835 Land Patent, Margaret Cross, Monroe, Michigan Territory

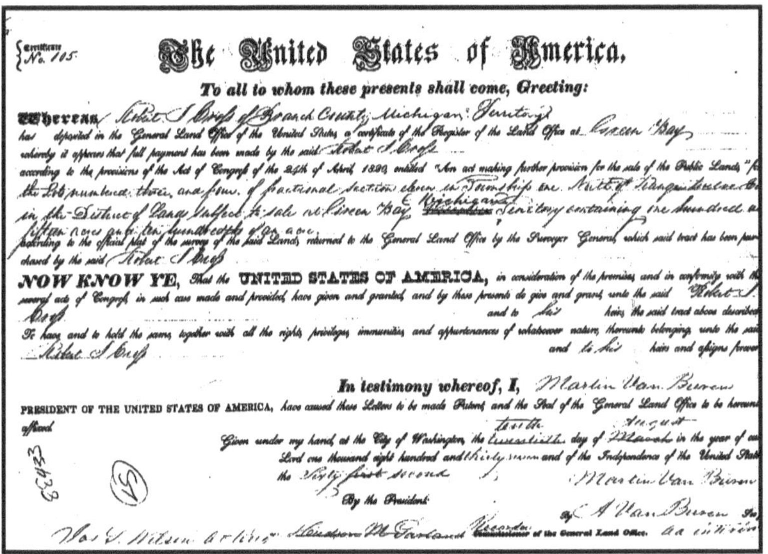

1837 Land Patent, Robert Cross; Branch Co., Michigan Territory

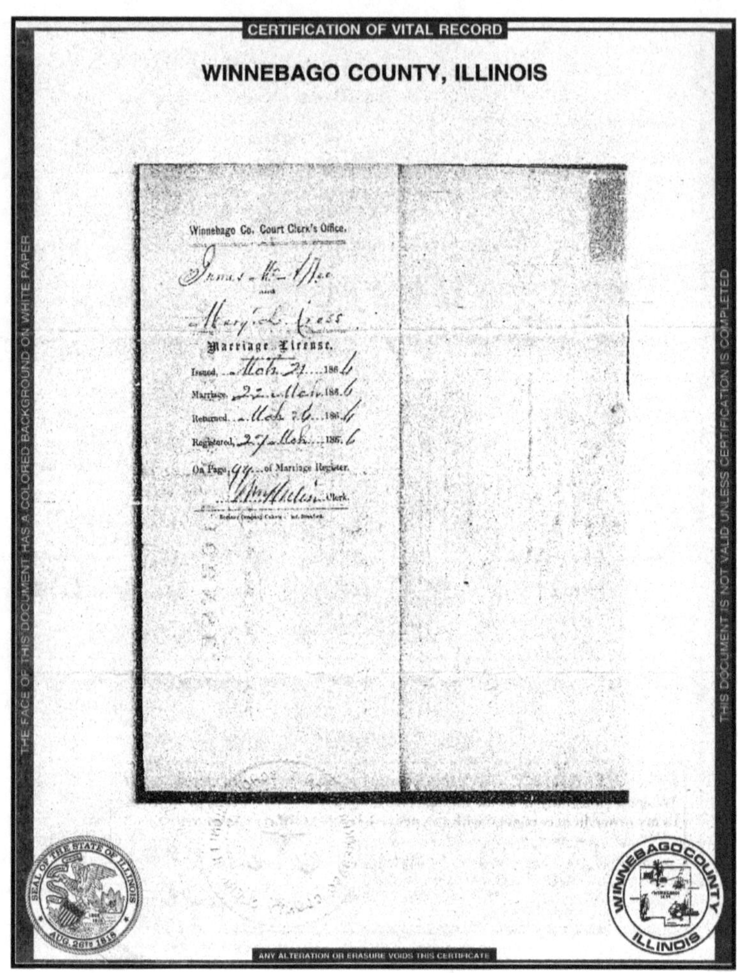

**Marriage License, James McAffee and Margaret Cross**

CERTIFICATION OF VITAL RECORD

# WINNEBAGO COUNTY, ILLINOIS

# MARRIAGE LICENSE.

*Office of the Clerk of the County Court.*

STATE OF ILLINOIS.
Winnebago County.

The People of the State of Illinois to all to whom these Presents shall come—GREETING:

BE IT KNOWN, That this LICENSE doth authorize any regular Minister of the Gospel, authorized to marry by the Church or Society to which he belongs, any Justice of the Supreme Court, Judge or Justice of the Peace, to celebrate and solemnize, within their County, the MARRIAGE of

according to law and the social customs.

WITNESS, William Hoolis, Clerk of the said County Court, and the seal of said Court, hereunto affixed, at Rockford, this __ day of __ in the year of our Lord One Thousand Eight Hundred and Sixty __.

William Hoolis, Clerk.

STATE OF ILLINOIS,
WINNEBAGO COUNTY.

GIVEN under my hand, this __ day of __ A. D. 186_.

State of Illinois, ss.
WINNEBAGO COUNTY,

The undersigned, __ of the County __ and State __ hereby applies to said Clerk for a License for the Marriage of __ with __ of the County __ and State __

And the said applicant, being duly sworn according to law, doth depose and say that the said male person, in whose behalf application for said License is made, is over the age of twenty-one years, and that the said female is over the age of eighteen years; and may lawfully contract and be joined in marriage.

ANY ALTERATION OR ERASURE VOIDS THIS CERTIFICATE

**Marriage License, James McAffee and Margaret Cross**

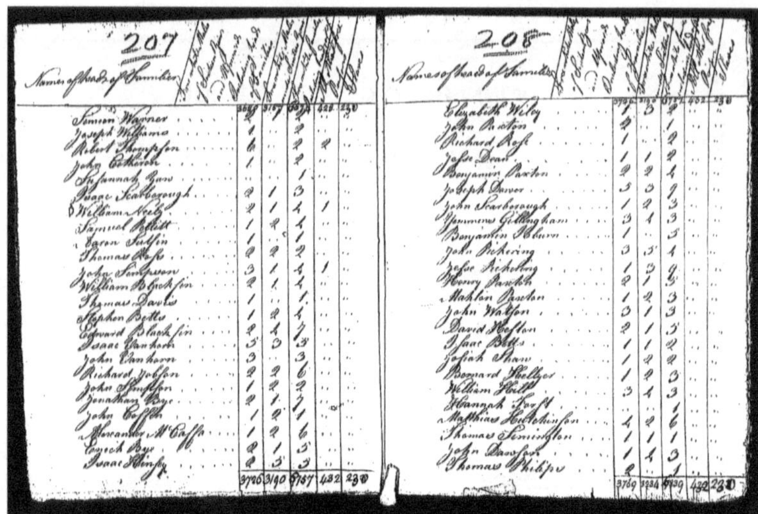

**Alexander McAffee in 1790 Bucks County, Pennsylvania Census.**

**James McAffee in Muster Roll**

1841 Land Patent,  Alexander McAffee, Winnebago Co., Illinois

the West half of The South West quarter of Section fourteen, in Township forty-five, of Range five, East, in the District of Lands subject to sale at Dixon, Illinois, containing eighty acres,



**1945 Land Patent of 2nd Great Grandfather Peter Ralston, on West Lane Road**

**1790 Northumberland, PA**

|  | | | | | |
|---|---|---|---|---|---|
| 20) James Harrison | 2 | 6 | 4 | | |
| William Gilmore | 2 | 2 | 3 | | |
| Benjamin Smith | 1 | 0 | 2 | | |
| William Hazlet | 1 | 3 | 4 | | |
| Joseph Lackens | 1 | | | | |
| Patrick Bhin | 2 | 1 | 5 | | |
| Patrick Dixon | 1 | 1 | 2 | | |
| James McAffee | 2 | 1 | 5 | | |
| And.s Cutbewit | 1 | | | | |
| John Tweed | 1 | 3 | 1 | | |
| James Bailey | 1 | 0 | 2 | | |
| David Bailey | 1 | 1 | 2 | | |
| Samuel Bailey | 1 | 0 | 4 | | |
| John Hart | 1 | 3 | 3 | | |
| Peter Dewe | 1 | 2 | 1 | | |
| James Cummins | 1 | 1 | 1 | | |
| Hugh Hamilton | 1 | 2 | 3 | | |
| Thomas Love | 1 | 0 | 4 | | |
| Jacob Langs sen'r | 1 | 0 | 1 | | |
| Jacob Langs jun'r | 1 | 1 | 1 | | |
| Anthony Sutton | 1 | 0 | 1 | | |
| Stephen Thimble | 1 | 1 | 4 | | |
| John Berret | 2 | 0 | 3 | | |
| James Neiley | 2 | 3 | 2 | | |
| Ezekiel Younglove | 1 | 2 | 6 | | |
| Perkins Lovel | 1 | 1 | 5 | | |
| Cushim & Thos Bedole | 2 | 0 | 2 | | |
| Jacob Morrels | 1 | 2 | 2 | | |
| Fleming Wilson | 3 | 2 | 5 | | |
| Charles McClung | 1 | 2 | 3 | | |
| Total | 39 | 40 | 81 | 0 | 0 |

|  | | | | | |
|---|---|---|---|---|---|
| Robert Shaw | 1 | 4 | 4 | 421 | |
| John Craig | 2 | 0 | 1 | | |
| Neal McCay | 3 | 3 | 3 | | |
| James McCay | 1 | | | | |
| Mary Mackey | 0 | 2 | 4 | | |
| And.w Anderson | 1 | 0 | 3 | | |
| Hugh Doeg | 1 | 2 | 4 | | |
| John Jingles | 1 | 0 | 1 | | |
| James Jingles | 1 | 1 | 1 | | |
| And.w Jingles | 1 | 2 | 3 | | |
| John Dixon | 2 | 0 | 3 | | |
| Daniel Wilson | 3 | 1 | 2 | | |
| Samuel Wilson | 1 | 3 | 4 | | |
| Hugh Lemond | 1 | 3 | 3 | | |
| Joseph McTharg | 1 | 1 | 4 | | |
| Benoni Wisener | 1 | 1 | 2 | | |
| Jesse Wisener | 2 | 1 | 4 | | |
| Widow Clemens | 0 | 1 | 3 | | |
| John Duart | 2 | 0 | 3 | | |
| Peter Smith | 1 | 2 | 2 | | |
| Samuel Curswell | 1 | 3 | 4 | | |
| Isaiah Fontson | 1 | 0 | 2 | | |
| John Fontson | 2 | 3 | 2 | | |
| Jas & John Linn | 2 | - | | | |
| George Wcandlish | 2 | 1 | 3 | | |
| Samuel Lowry | 1 | 0 | 1 | | |
| John Strawbrige | 1 | 1 | 2 | | |
| Matthew Crozier | 1 | 5 | 2 | | |
| Joseph Henderson | 1 | | | | |
| John Cox | 1 | 4 | 4 | | |
| Total | 39 | 44 | 74 | 0 | 0 |

**1790 Northumberland, PA**

3rd Great Grandfather James McAffee; 1790 U S Census, Northumberland County, Pennsylvania

2nd Great Grandfather Robert J Cross; 1860 U S Census, Roscoe, Illinois

Great Grandmother Jane Ralston certificate, April 1923

1766 Marriage record; Old Swede Church, Phila, PA.;  4th Great
Grandparents Alexander McMichael and Martha Johnson

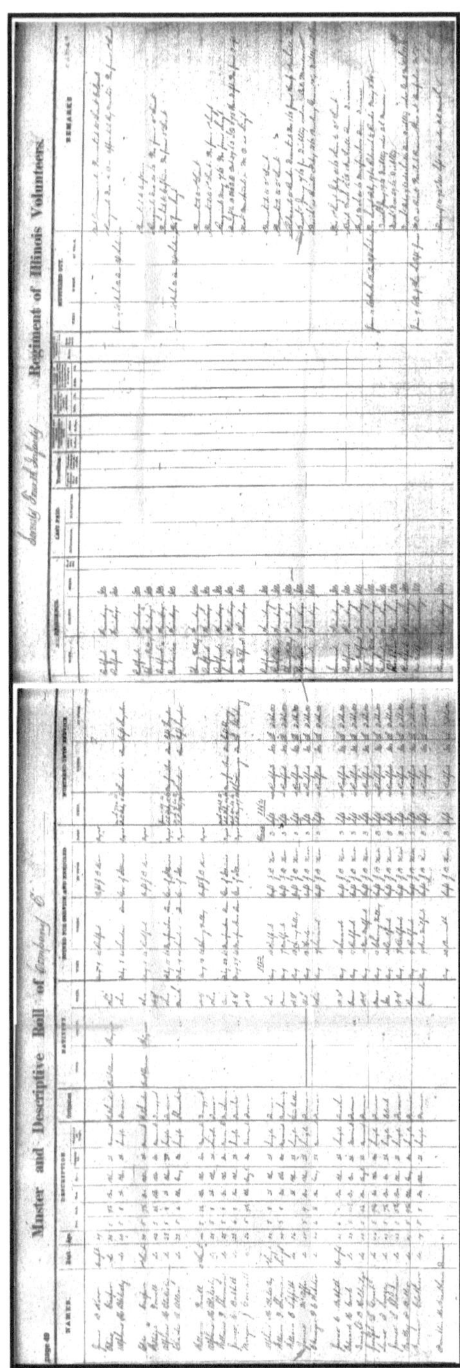

Muster Roll Co. E, 74 Regiment of Illinois; Great Grandfather James
McAffee; August 13, 1862; Rockford, Illinois

Marriage license; Great Grandparents Thomas and Jane Ralston, April 2, 1857; Boone Co., Illinois

Mr. and Mrs. James McAffee

request you to be present

at the marriage of their daughter

Hannah J

to

P. William Ralston,

Thursday Evening, November 6th, 1890,

*

at 8-30 o'clock.

Roscoe,        Illinois

**1890 Wedding Invitation, Hannah J McAffee and P William Ralston**

**Marriage license; Grandparents Peter W Ralston and Hannah J McAffee, November 6, 1890, Roscoe, Illinois**

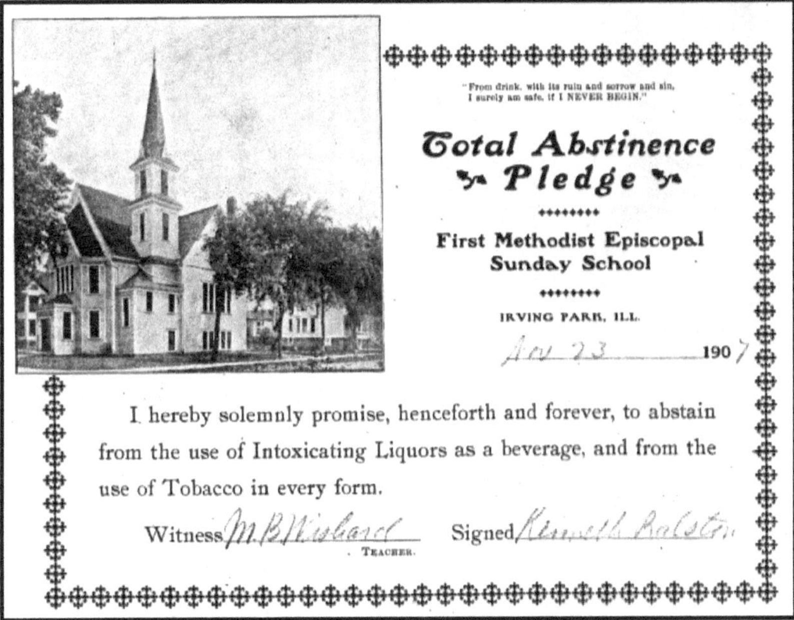


1907 Abstinence pledge, Kenneth M Ralston



Peter W Ralston Engineer member and business cards, 1927

# Artifacts-

Grandpa Peter Ralston shaving mug

Wooden Pot used by Grandpa Peter Ralston to carry sugar from Roscoe, Illinois, grocery store

'Psalms and Hymns', belonging to
Great Grandmother Jean/Jane Ralston

Inside of cover, 'Mrs Jean Ralston
Hymn Book Jan 14th 1859'

Mrs Jane McCarty
McAffee Psalms (wife of
Alexander)

'Presented to Mrs. McAffee on her 71st
Birthday from a Friend, April 6 1871' and next
page has her signature 'Mrs. Jane McAffee'

**McAffee Table; bought by Hannah Benedict Cross about 1850**

**Burns Club 1884 Annual Picnic; Rockford, Illinois**

James M McAffee Gate-Leg table; made from Roscoe, Illinois, Cross farm, walnut log; about 1870

Library table made in high school by Kenneth M Ralston about 1910

# Maps-

"Plat of Survey made by me for Mssrs. Alexander and John McAffee (brothers) in Section No. 4 in Township No. Forty Five of North Range & East of 3rd principle Meridian. Ferguson Surveyor 18th July 1842". ( John has 50.74 and Alexander has 152.23 acres)

**1871 Roscoe map with Robert J Cross and J McAffee land**

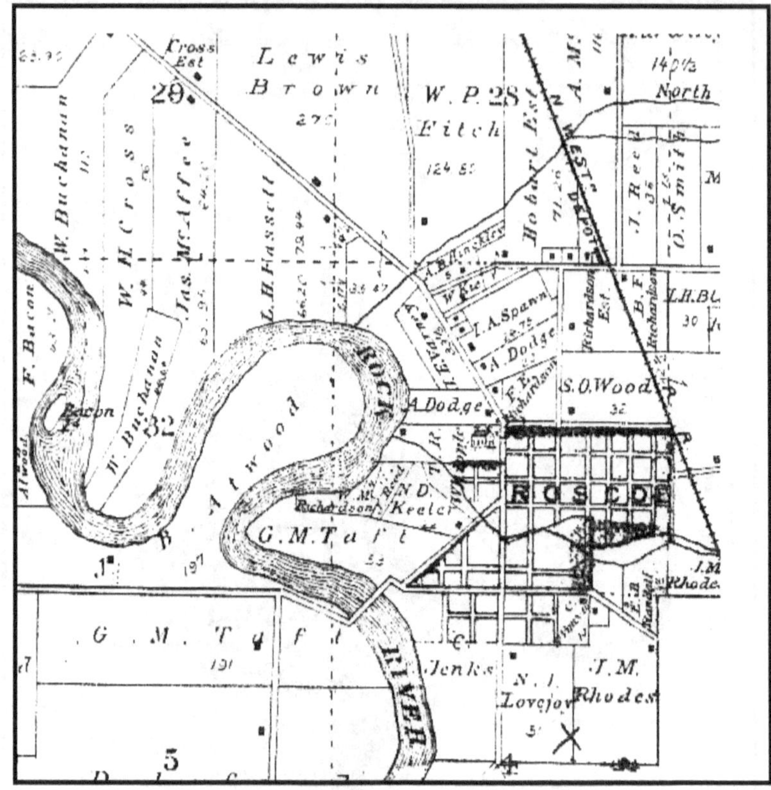


**1884 Roscoe map with Cross Est. , W H Cross, and Jas. McAffee land**

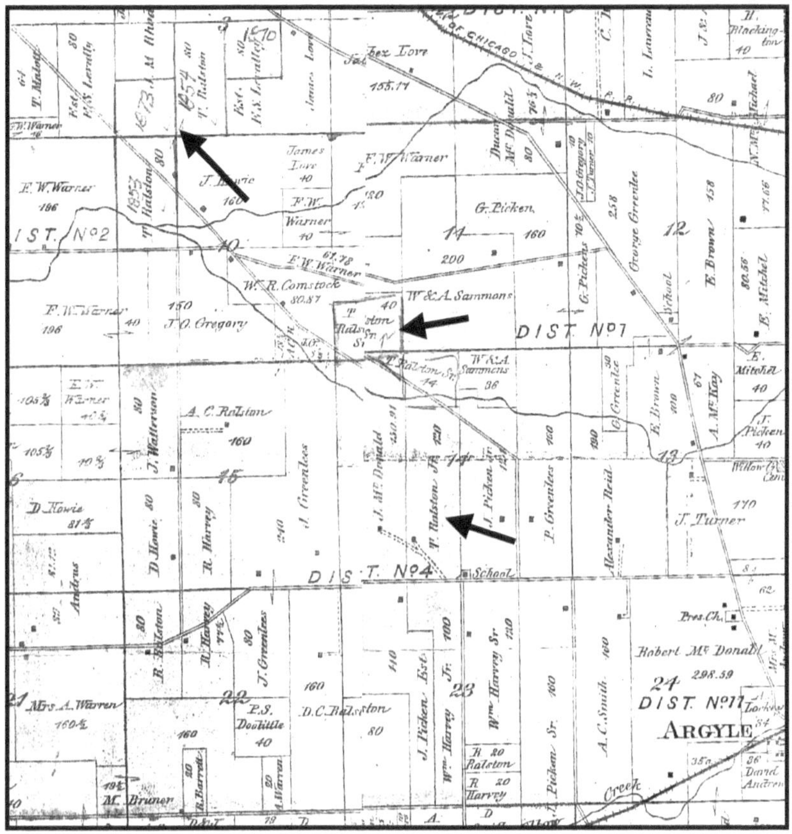

1871 map near Argyle with T Ralston Sr. and T Ralston Jr. land

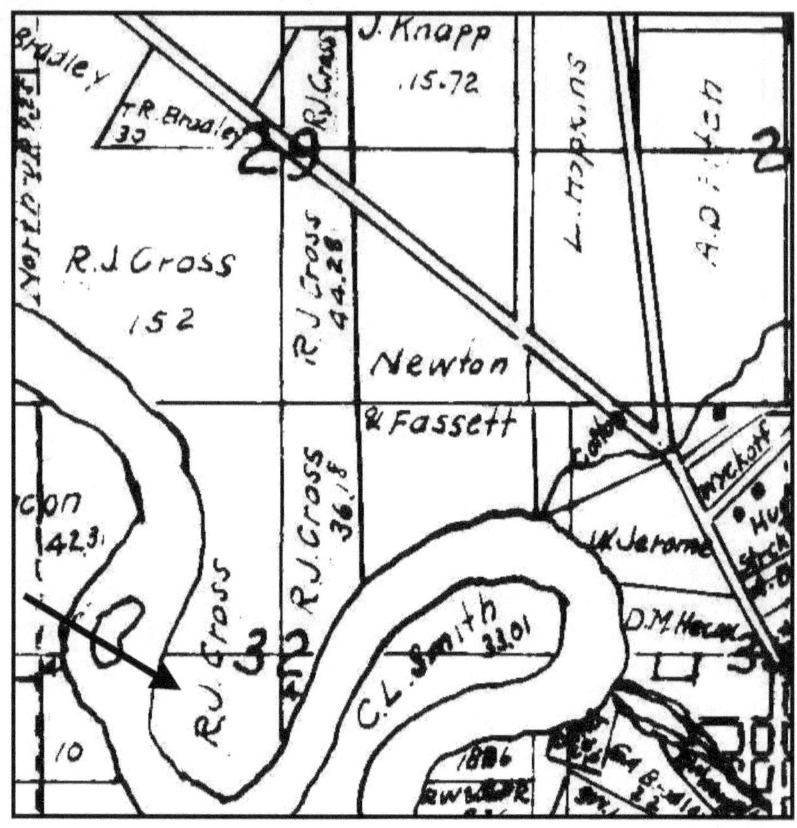



**R J Cross farm by Rock River, Roscoe, Illinois, about 1859**

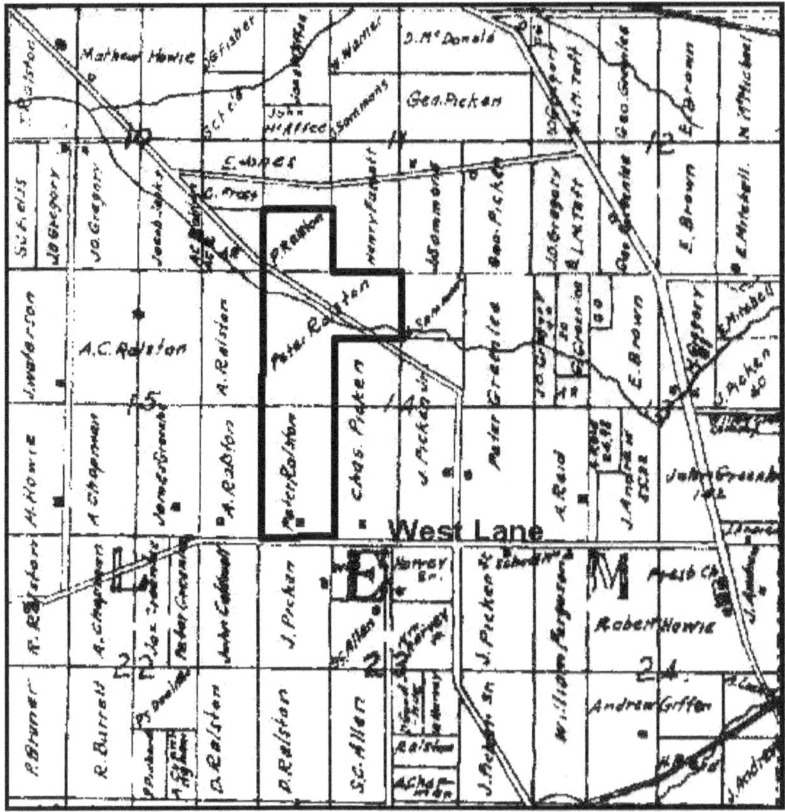

**2nd Great Grandfather Peter Ralston farm on West Lane road, about 1859**

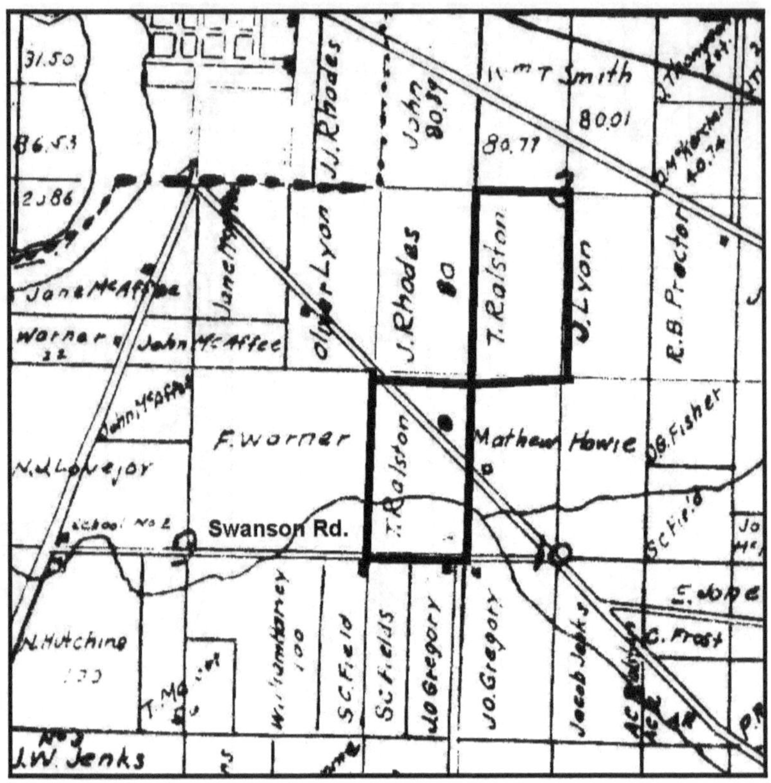


**Great Grandfather Thomas Ralston farm on McDonald road, near Roscoe, Illinois about 1859**

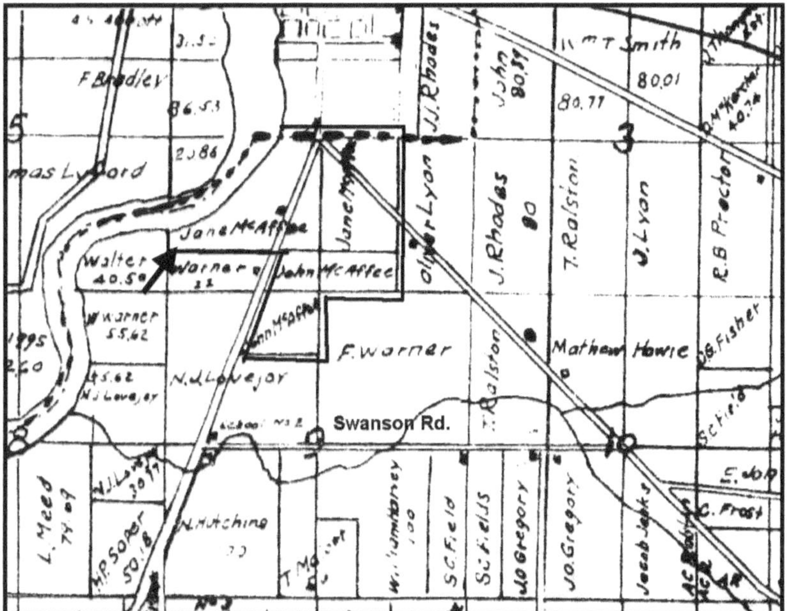


**Second Great Grandmother Jane McCarty and McAffee farm by Rock River, near Roscoe, Illinois, about 1859**

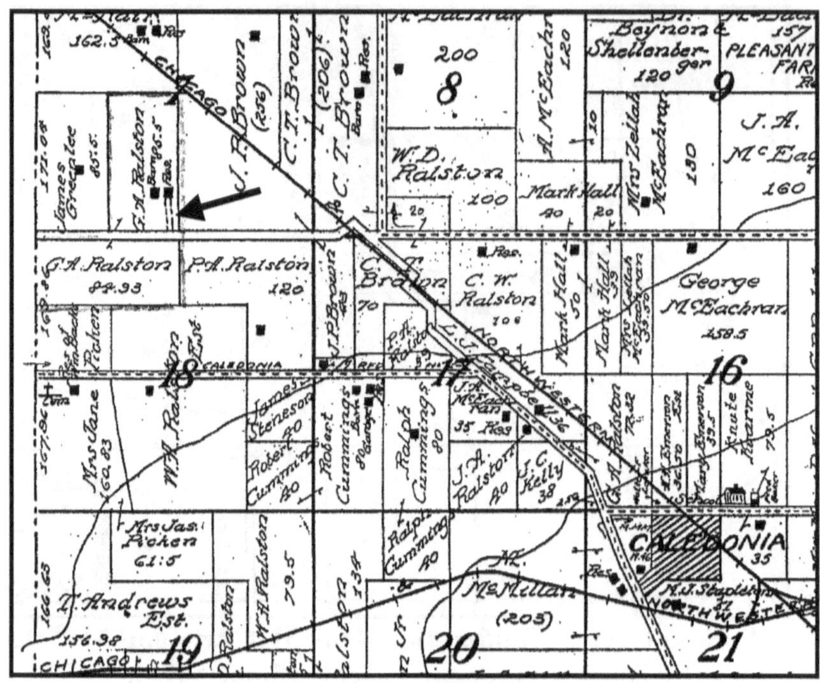


**1923 Caledonia map; 2nd cousin G A Ralston at 2nd Great Grandfather John Ralston farm location**

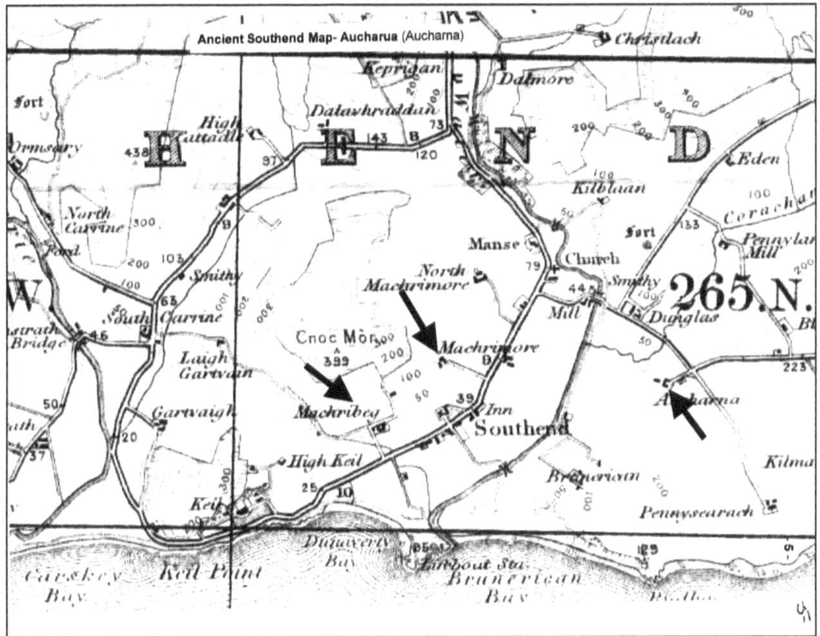



Map of Southend Parish, Kintyre; with Aucharua, 1835 birthplace of Gr-Grandmother Jane Ralston; Machrimore, 1820 home of 3rd Gr-Grandfather Charles Brown; Machribeg, birth of 2nd Gr-Grandmother Isabelle Greenlee

For Internet map of Kintyre, Scotland, go to- http://tinyurl.com/lmpa95w

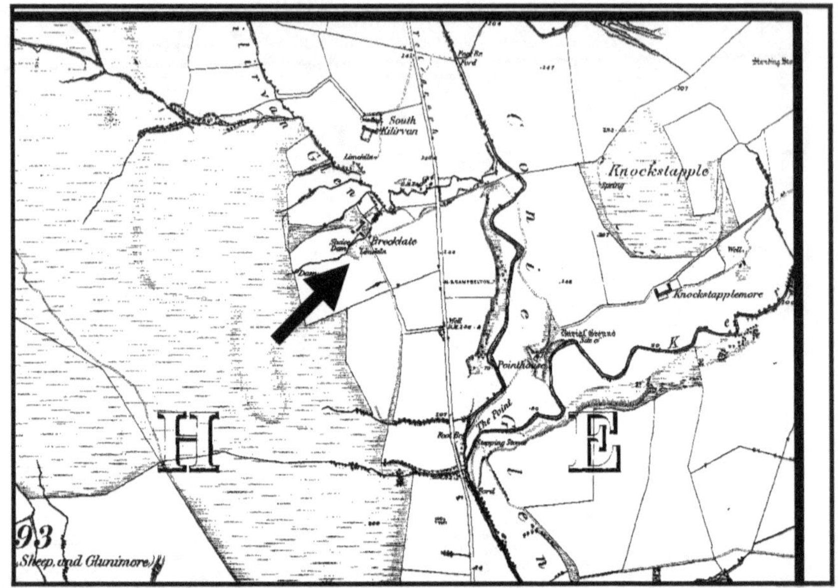


**Brecklate Farm, Southend, Kintyre, Scotland. Birthplace of GrGrGreatGrandfather John Ralston 1772**

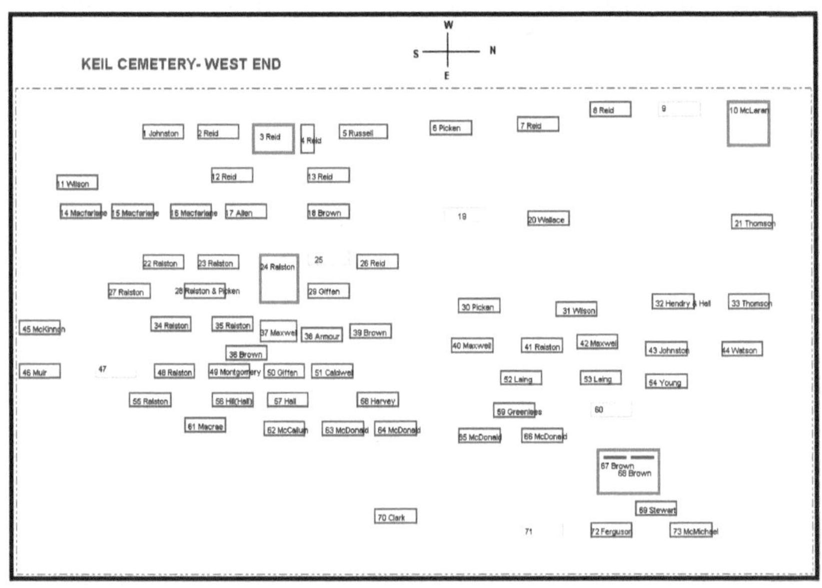


**Southend Cemetery, Kintyre, Scotland**

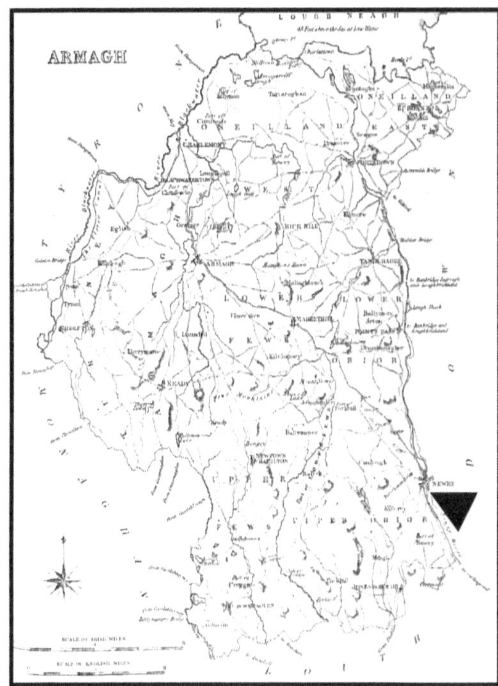

**Newry, Armagh, Northern Ireland; Home of 3rd Great-Grandmother Margaret Hanna Connelly about 1786 when she married Rev. John Cross**

See:  http://www.ralstongenealogy.com/45mrghan.htm

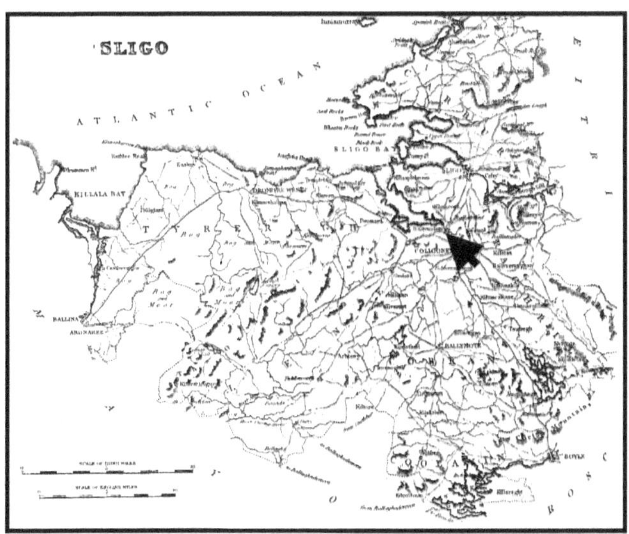

**Sligo, Northern Ireland; home of 3rd Great-Grandparents John and Margaret Hanna Connelly Cross about 1798, before going to America**

# Robert J Cross Park and Home

Roscoe Township has a public park named for Robert J Cross, dedicated in October 2018.

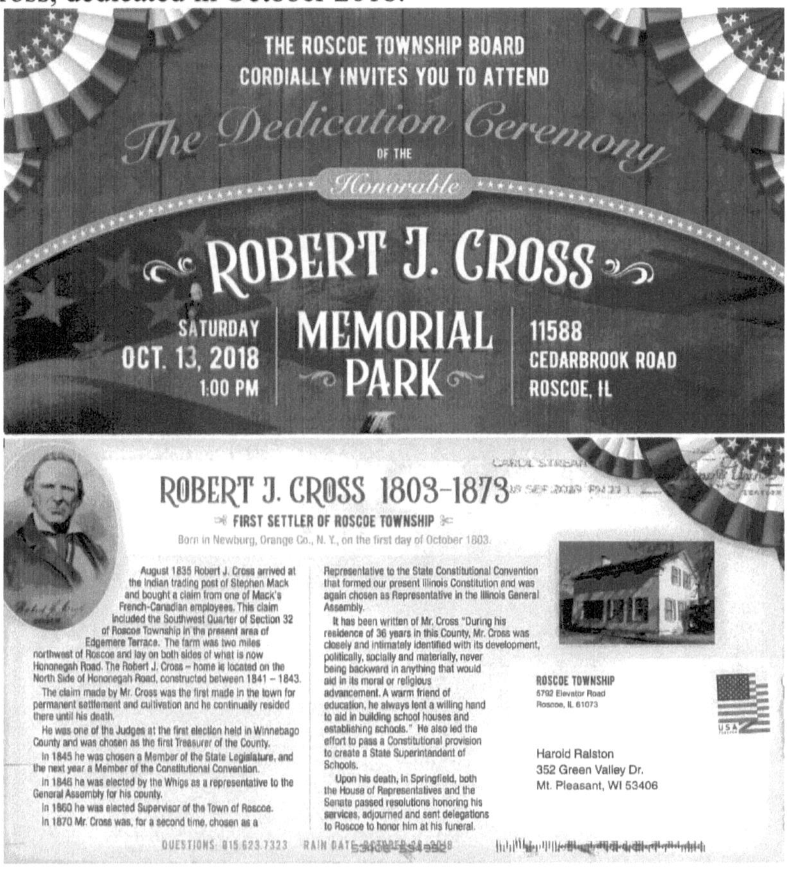



Invitation to dedication ceremony

Plaque at park

The Roscoe Township Historical Society has plans to use the restored family home of Robert J Cross as an historical museum.

**Cross home about 1940**

**Proposed Roscoe Township Museum**

# My other books

Printed by Lulu Press-
- 1916-1918 Letters to Kenneth McAffee Ralston, 79 pages, 2018, Lulu Press
- J I Case Pioneer Engineers and their Patents 1871-1943, 204 pages, 2018, Lulu Press
- Roscoe, Illinois Area Inventors 1867 – 1910, 168 pages, 2018, Lulu Press
- Emerson Manufacturing Co., A Family Connection, 138 pages, 2019, Lulu Press
- Emerson Manufacturing, the Abraham Lincoln Connection, 206 pages, 2019, Lulu Press
- Family Photograph Albums 1855-1910, 134 pages. Color print, 2019, Lulu Press
- Wisconsin Ancestry of Evelyn Belden Ralston, 172 pages, Color print or black & white 2019, Lulu Press

The above may be purchased at -
http://www.lulu.com/spotlight/haroldar